FIELD DRESSING AND BUTCHERING

Upland Birds, Waterfowl, and Wild Turkeys

Books by Monte Burch

Field Dressing and Butchering Rabbits, Squirrels, and Other Small Game
Field Dressing and Butchering Deer
Field Dressing and Butchering Big Game
The Field & Stream All-Terrain-Vehicle Handbook
Denny Brauer's Jig Fishing Secrets
Denny Brauer's Winning Tournament Tactics
Black Bass Basics
Guide to Calling & Rattling Whitetail Bucks
Guide to Successful Turkey Calling
Guide to Calling & Decoying Waterfowl
Guide to Successful Predator Calling
Pocket Guide to Seasonal Largemouth Bass Patterns
Pocket Guide to Seasonal Walleye Tactics
Pocket Guide to Old Time Catfish Techniques
Pocket Guide to Field Dressing, Butchering & Cooking Deer
Pocket Guide to Bowhunting Whitetail Deer
Pocket Guide to Spring & Fall Turkey Hunting
Truman Guide to Fishing, Hunting & Camping
The Pro's Guide to Fishing Missouri Lakes
Waterfowling, A Sportsman's Handbook
Modern Waterfowl Hunting
Shotgunner's Guide
Gun Care and Repair
Outdoorsman's Fix-It Book
Outdoorsman's Workshop
Building and Equipping the Garden and Small Farm Workshop
Basic House Wiring
Complete Guide to Building Log Homes
Children's Toys and Furniture
64 Yard and Garden Projects You Can Build
How to Build 50 Classic Furniture Reproductions
Tile Indoors and Out
The Home Cabinetmaker
How to Build Small Barns & Outbuildings
Masonry & Concrete
Pole Building Projects
Building Small Barns, Sheds & Shelters
Home Canning & Preserving (w/Joan Burch)
Building Mediterranean Furniture (w/Jay Hedden)
Fireplaces w/Robert Jones
The Homeowners Complete Manual of Repair and Improvement (w/3 others)
The Good Earth Almanac Series
Survival Handbook
Old Time Recipes
Natural Gardening Handbook

FIELD DRESSING AND BUTCHERING
Upland Birds, Waterfowl, and Wild Turkeys

Step-by-Step Instructions, from Field to Table

Monte Burch

The Lyons Press
Guilford, CT
An imprint of The Globe Pequot Press

The Lyons Press is an imprint of The Globe Pequot Press.

Printed in the United States of America

10 9 8 7 6 5 4 3

Library of Congress Cataloging-in-Publication Data is available on
file.

Contents

Introduction

The last rays of sun dip below the horizon as the hunters trudge slowly back from fields and marshes, the day's hunt ended. For some hunters, the better part of the day indeed ends with the last shots. They groan inwardly at the thought of the work involved in cleaning their kill and think seriously about avoiding the dreaded task by giving the day's work away. The end of the day doesn't need be that way. With the right equipment—plus a little skill and patience—the pleasure of the day afield can be extended into delicious meals that you, your family, and your friends will enjoy, giving you double pleasure by providing nutritious and healthful food for the table.

One of my quail-hunting partners ends the day with panache. At the end of the hunt, after the dogs have been kenneled into the trailer, Harry brings out a small flask of brandy and a set of crystal glasses and pours a shot for each hunter. He gives a salute to his favorite game and then proceeds to efficiently dress the birds in the waning evening light. Not only is this a fitting tribute to a great game bird and an enjoyed hunt, but when he gets home the work is done and he can relax or meet his social engagements without hassle.

Wildfowl have been a mainstay food source from the beginning of mankind. Fowl can be prepared and cooked as simply as wrapping a whole bird in clay and baking in the coals of a campfire, or with elegant recipes featured in the world's most famous resorts and restaurants.

North America is blessed with an abundance of wildfowl, with upland birds, waterfowl, and turkeys being the three major groupings. Upland birds include blue, spruce, and ruffed grouse; woodcock; and rock, white-tailed, and willow ptarmigan in the North. Greater and lesser prairie chickens, sharp-tailed and sage grouse, and Hungarian partridges comprise the primary plains game birds. The bobwhite quail is the only major game bird in the South, but

Wildfowl—including upland birds, waterfowl, and wild turkeys—provide some of the most pleasurable days afield and some of the finest of foods.

other quail found across the country include mountain, Gambel's, scaled, Montezuma, and California. Add wild chukars, found mostly in the West, the ubiquitous ring-necked pheasant, and doves (found in most of the country and clearly the most popular game bird in America), and you have a remarkable lineup of tasty table fare.

The wild turkey, meanwhile, has made a remarkable comeback throughout much of its native range, as well as in many nonnative places. This is due to extensive management by state game departments, along with lots of help from the Wild Turkey Federation and its many local chapters.

The wide variety of waterfowl includes numerous species of ducks: mallard; gadwall; northern pintail; blue-winged, cinnamon, and green-winged teal; Eurasian and American widgeon; fulvous whistling duck; northern shoveler; wood duck; canvasback; redhead; ring-necked; greater and lesser scaup or bluebill; common and Barrow's goldeneye; bufflehead; old squaw; harlequin; king eider; black scoter; surf scoter; white-winged scoter; ruddy duck; and hooded, common, and red-breasted merganser. Goose species include Canada, brant, white-fronted, snow, and Ross'. Other waterfowl include the sandhill crane, rail, and snipe.

Some of the more desirable game birds were once hunted by market hunters and sold to the city markets. In fact, a few of these species were gunned almost to extinction in the late 1800s. Fortunately, regulations demanded by sport hunters, along with proper management, allowed many of these game birds to rebound to the point they are now, more abundant than ever.

Most wildfowl hunters revere their favorite game and carefully dress the birds and prepare the meat. A variety of dressing methods can be used for each fowl, depending on the field conditions, age and sex of the bird, and the method of cooking to be used. Wildfowl can be plucked or skinned, left whole, quartered, breasted, or cut into small pieces, all depending on the recipe to be used as well as the age of the bird. Some recipes call for a specific dressing method. This book covers all of the dressing techniques you'll need, plus has tips on preparing, preserving, and cooking all of the various wildfowl.

I grew up on a Missouri farm where quail hunting was a way of life. So was waterfowling. Living in one of the best spots on the Mississippi flyway, I've been hunting ducks and geese for as long as I can remember. Missouri was also one of the first states to manage wild turkeys, and these days our Ozarks farm is home to numerous birds, providing not only Thanksgiving but Christmas and other dinners as well.

I've also been fortunate to hunt wildfowl throughout much of North America. I'm always interested in tips and recipes provided by my hosts, guides, and other "locals." A number of recipes are included in the book. My wife, Joan, and I have developed many of these recipes over the years. Some are from friends and relatives; others come from a few of the many places I've been fortunate enough to hunt.

CHAPTER 1

Tools and Equipment

Having the proper tools and equipment for field dressing and processing wildfowl is critical. A good, clean work space for cutting up and preparing the birds is also important. The tools, equipment, and work space needed depends on the amount of field dressing and butchering you do and the types of game birds involved.

CUTTING AND SHARPENING TOOLS

Many upland birders prefer to draw or eviscerate game birds in the field, especially when hunting in hot climates where the meat can spoil quickly. A sharp pocketknife with a gut hook makes the chore easy on small birds, such as quail and grouse.

Knives are available in a variety of steels, ranging from stainless steel through several grades of carbon steel and combinations of steel. Stainless-steel knives are the hardest, with soft-carbon steel the softest. Stainless steel requires a great deal more effort to sharpen but holds the edge longer than the carbon metals. I prefer a stainless-steel knife for field dressing but use carbon-steel knives for butchering. I don't have to worry about the stainless-steel field-dressing knife becoming dull while on a hunt, and it doesn't rust from blood stains if it's not immediately cleaned and dried properly. The carbon butcher knives, on the other hand, allow for quick touch-ups with a steel or hone during the butchering process.

Regardless of the type of knife and metal, it's extremely important to have the knife as sharp as possible when field dressing, skinning, or cutting up birds. In fact, when skinning and cutting up birds

Having the proper tools is important in properly dressing and preparing wildfowl. Many hunters prefer to draw or gut game birds in the field. A pocketknife with a gut hook makes the chore easy.

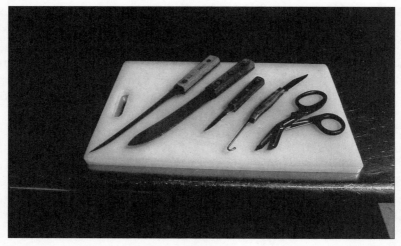

Knives for cutting up the birds at home or camp are also necessary, the type and size depending on the type and size of birds. You'll need a range of butcher knives, from small paring knife size to larger knives for slicing.

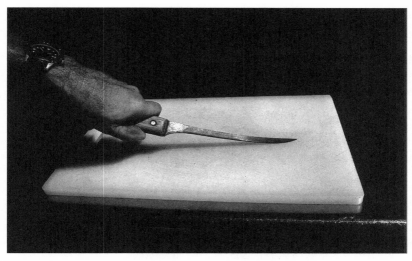

Above all else, a good boning knife is critical. The knife should have a thin, flexible blade that can be slid and bent around bones. A flexible fish fillet knife can also be used.

at home, I keep several knives sharpened and ready to use so I don't have to stop and sharpen or hone a blade during the process.

A wide variety of sharpening devices are available, ranging from simple handheld stones to electric grinding wheels. My grandfather's old foot-turned grinding wheel did a great job of sharpening knives, and many of today's electric wheels offer the same degree of sharpening.

A pair of Chef'sChoice game shears are extremely handy. They can be used to quickly clip off the feet, wings, and heads of game birds and to split the carcass if desired. Game/kitchen shears are particularly handy when dressing quail and other small game birds.

Cutting surfaces are also important. Although wooden cutting boards are traditional, they are more difficult to clean and sanitize than some of the newer surfaces. Once wooden cutting boards become deeply grooved from knives, it's especially hard to completely remove blood and meat particles. The best cutting surfaces don't become grooved with knife cuts and can be easily cleaned and sanitized. Also make sure the surface you choose doesn't dull your knife blade too quickly. It's a good idea to have one large surface,

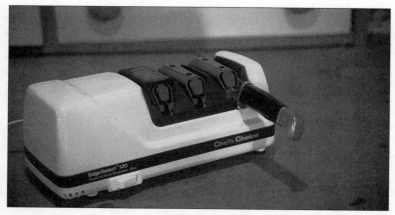

Knife-sharpening tools are another necessity. These can range from the traditional butcher's sharpening steel to a variety of stones and even electric hones such as the Chef'sChoice model shown.

or at least a couple of smaller ones. My dad ran a cabinet shop for years, and we recycled the plastic laminate sink cutouts as cutting boards. These work great but still become damaged over time and should be replaced.

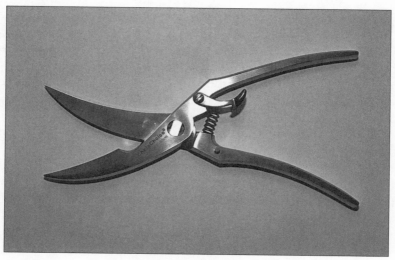

Game shears are perfect for clipping wings, feet, and heads.

Other tools include pans for holding dressed birds, cutting boards for cutting and preparing, grinder/slicers, and vacuum wrappers.

WORK SPACE

You can, of course, skin, dress, or prepare wildfowl on your kitchen table or counter. It's a messy chore at best, and feathers tend to drift everywhere. A space set aside for the chore—outside or in a garage or outbuilding—is best. This space doesn't have to be elaborate nor involve a lot of area, and you can use the area for other endeavors when it's not needed for game cleaning.

You'll need a sturdy table with an easily cleanable top. This can be a plastic laminate top, or you can simply use a disposable oil cloth or plastic tablecloth for butchering if the tabletop is made of wood. One of the best surfaces is stainless steel. It hoses down and cleans up easily, and is sturdy and hard surfaced. You will still need a separate cutting surface over the stainless steel, as the steel will scratch and quickly dull knife blades. Several years ago I bought two used stainless-steel school cafeteria kitchen tables at an auction, and they have turned out to be one of my best investments. I have one set up outside next to my garage with a work light over it and an outside plug and hose nearby. I use this area for everything from filleting fish to dressing wild turkeys and waterfowl to cutting up deer. I have the other table set up in my garage for protection from the weather and for those days when it's too hot or too cold to do butchering chores outside. Both of the tables are at a comfortable, 36-inch-high working height. Low tables can cause back problems when grinding or cutting up meat in a slightly bent-over position. If you want to buy a butchering table, Game Locker carries stainless-steel models as well as other butchering supplies.

OTHER TOOLS

In some instances, wildfowl is field dressed, skinned, or hung, either in the field or at home. A game belt to hold the birds properly by the neck is extremely handy. The best place to hang birds is out of the sun in a shaded but well-ventilated area.

Game birds should be kept cool from the moment they're taken, and that means keeping them in a cooler with ice on hot days or making sure your game vest has plenty of ventilation. I also use an old refrigerator to hold field-dressed game birds, especially turkeys, for a couple of days before butchering them. I think this has some of the same benefits as hanging big game in cool lockers.

Other items you'll need include pans to hold meat as you butcher. Large plastic tubs can be used to hold meat cuts for grinding. Lots of clean, soft rags are also important for wiping and cleaning your hands, cleaning surfaces, and removing feathers from knife blades and hands.

Dark-meat geese can be ground and made into sausage. To do this, you'll need a meat grinder. Hand-cranked grinders can be used, but they must be good-quality meat grinders, not the smaller, economical kitchen grinders. If you intend to make sausage, you'll need a grinder with two blades—⅜- and ³⁄₁₆-inch blades, or ⅜- and ¼-inch blades. Electric-powered grinders are available in various sizes, depending on the amount of meat to be ground, and range from about 2 pounds to 5 pounds per minute for commercial-grade models.

I was lucky enough to inherit an old grinder from my granddad. The grinder was actually run off the back wheel shaft of a Model A when granddad had it. My dad eventually hooked an electric motor to it. "Better not have your tie in the grinder when you turn it on," was granddad's favorite saying. It really works. New grinders do

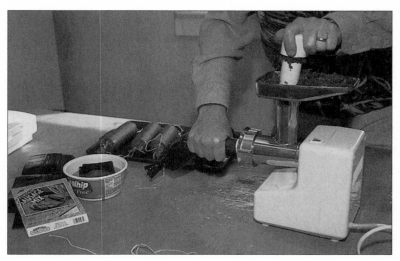

If you intend to make sausage from dark-meated birds, such as snow geese, you'll need a grinder with a sausage stuffer.

have benefits, however, coming not only with a variety of blades but also sausage stuffers, which allow you to grind and stuff sausage casings at the same time. The Sausage Maker carries a number of grinding and stuffing products, as does Cabela's and Bass Pro Shops.

A butane torch will singe the fine "hairs" from plucked birds, and a mechanical plucker could be a consideration if you dress a lot of waterfowl. Another handy item is an electric food slicer which is great for slicing large quantities of meat for jerky. A dehydrator also makes short work of drying jerky, and a vacuum packing system, such as the FoodSaver, provides the best method of preparing meat for freezing.

Dressing Upland Game Birds

Fighting my way through a solid mass of tangled moonseed vines, I spotted the still-white form of Rebel, my English setter. "Point," I yelled to my hunting partner.

"Take care of yourself, I've got one over here," came the answering shout.

After an agonizing struggle through the thorns, panting with exertion and wearing a great deal less skin, I finally got within a few yards of Rebel. I still had a tremendous brush pile between us when I heard the pop of my partner's 20 gauge. At the sound, Rebel rolled her eyes toward me, her only movement. I hesitated, then bulldozed through the brush pile, past Rebel, and swung on the fast-ris-

Upland game birds, such as pheasant, quail, or grouse, can provide exquisite meals ranging from simple smoked or grilled birds to dinners satisfying the most discriminating gourmet.

ing quail, only to take out a tree limb a foot behind the bird's eva-
sive flight pattern in the dense thicket. While I was contemplating
my good shooting, two more birds thundered from behind, and in
an almost impossible side swing, I toppled the first bird and
watched the other fly straight across the creek and land within 100
yards of where we stood. I picked up my bird and carefully placed
the small, warm body in the back of my game vest.

My partner came up holding a nice cock and grinning. "Got a
whipping on that one, eh? Guess where they all went?" He pointed
across the water to the opposite shore.

"It's a 2-mile hike before we can cross the creek," I replied. "But
we don't have a choice, do we?"

Upland game birds are the epitome of sporting shooting. They
afford great challenges and pleasures in the field and on the table.
They are the perfect birds with which to begin this book.

FIELD CARE

Regardless of whether you prefer to dress your game afield or at
home, how you take care of your game while in the field makes a
great deal of difference to the final results. This is especially true in
hot weather. Dove and quail taken in the early part of the season—
when the temperatures can soar above the 90s in the South, West,
and even some parts of the Midwest—should be carefully handled
to prevent spoilage.

Field care of doves is simple because you're often sitting in one
spot. A cooler filled with ice can easily be carried to most dove
blinds; simply toss the birds into the cooler as you collect them.
Most states require that individuals keep their birds separated. If
you're hunting with a buddy, use labeled plastic zipper bags so
both of you can use the same cooler.

Quail, pheasants, and other upland game should be carried in a
mesh game pouch or vest that allows for full air circulation, not in a
rubber-lined vest. Or, you can hang the birds on your belt if the
weather is extremely hot. Eviscerating birds as soon as they're collected also helps in cooling birds in hot climates.

Dove and other game birds can also be dressed in the field, but
make sure you follow game rules and regulations. In many instances you will have to leave one wing with the feathers intact and

Game birds should be kept as cool as possible while in the field. Use a cooler if you're sitting in one spot and hunting birds such as doves. If you're walking and carrying birds, use a mesh game vest that allows for good air circulation.

sometimes evidence of the bird's sex. These rules apply to game in the field or during transport.

Regardless of when you plan to dress the bird, a 3-second evisceration job will make later chores easier. Bend back the breast and

Puncture the belly skin and use a gut-hook knife to eviscerate

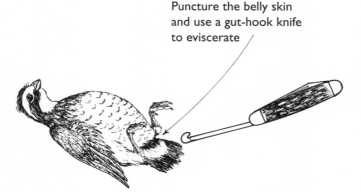

Drawing or eviscerating game birds in the field can also help cool the carcass and prevent spoiling in hot weather. On small birds, such as quail, simply pinch the belly skin to break it, and use your finger or a knife with a gut hook to pull out the entrails. Keep paper towels in your pocket for cleaning your hands.

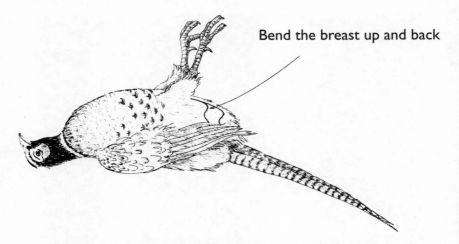

Bend the breast up and back

On larger birds, such as grouse or pheasants, bend the breast up and back.

make a cut just under the breastbone to the vent; with small birds such as quail, you can simply use your finger to push through the thin stomach muscle. Then use the gut hook of the knife to pull out the entrails. Incidentally, if you don't have a knife with a gut hook, you can make one in the field with a forked stick, or simply use

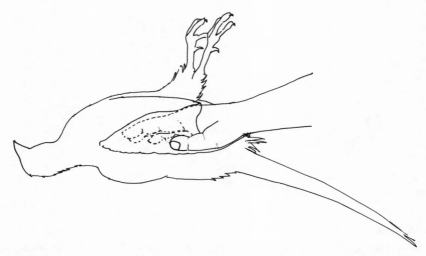

Make a cut across the belly skin, then down each side of the anus. Remove the entrails with your fingers.

your fingers. It's best to carry a package of moist wipes or a clean rag with you to the field for cleanup after eviscerating your birds.

TRANSPORTING AND COOLING BIRDS

The most important factor in getting good-quality meat from game birds is to cool them quickly, and to keep them cool. If you don't, the delicate meat can easily spoil. If transporting the birds in your automobile, use a cooler with ice to keep birds cool. Even in cold weather, spread the birds out loosely in the trunk of the vehicle rather than piling them up in a corner or leaving them in a game vest. Be sure to follow all state game laws pertaining to transporting your birds.

Some hunters hang their birds for a couple of days to cure before they prepare them to eat or freeze them for later use. In either case, the bird must be eviscerated ahead of time.

Once the birds have been plucked, skinned, and dressed, soak them in salt water overnight in the refrigerator. This will help remove the blood clotting around wounds. Pick off any feathers, remove any visible shot, and cut away any bloody areas before preparing for the table or freezer.

QUAIL

Fried quail and potatoes and gravy are often the mouthwatering result of an invigorating and pleasant day afield. Two popular methods can be used for dressing quail, and the method chosen depends on how the quail are to be cooked. In most instances, quail are skinned rather than plucked, and it takes less than a minute for an experienced hand to skin and dress a quail. All you'll need is a sharp pocketknife and a pair of game shears.

The first step is to remove the head. This can be done with game shears or by using a simple pulling and twisting motion. The wings are then removed by twisting them off at the base of the breast or by using game shears or a sharp knife. Be careful of cut or broken wing bones, which can be extremely sharp and can easily slice or stab your hand. Next, using game shears, remove the bottom portion of the legs at the joint where the feathers and shin join;

Dressing quail is quick and easy. The first step is to remove the head and both wings by twisting off or cutting off with game shears or a sharp knife.

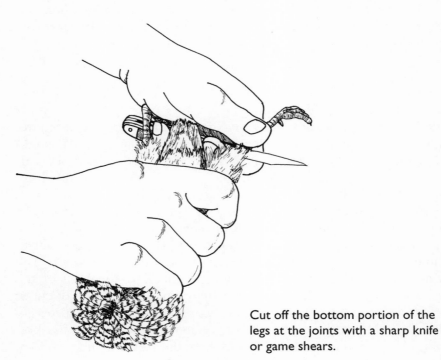

Cut off the bottom portion of the legs at the joints with a sharp knife or game shears.

With the tail of the quail pointing away from you, grasp belly skin and pull up. Peel the rest of the skin away from the bird. Pull away the crop.

or remove them by bending them backward to snap the joint, then cutting through the joint with a knife. Hold the carcass with the tail pointing away from you, grasp the belly skin, and pull upward toward the head. The skin will peel away easily. Continue peeling away the rest of the skin and feathers. Pull away the crop, examine it to determine what the birds have been eating, then discard it.

If the bird was eviscerated in the field, simply cut off the tail at the base of the spine. If the birds have not been field dressed, pull the breast backward and use your finger to push through the belly muscle, then dig out the entrails with your finger. Allow the entrails to remain attached to the vent, and cut off the tail and vent with the entrails attached. Place the carcass in cold water.

Quail dressed in this manner can be cooked in one piece or further separated into two pieces: the breast and the leg section. The leg section is spread apart until it pops at the backbone, making for easier frying. My mom used to fry the breasts for the evening meal, but the legs added a "delicacy" to breakfast.

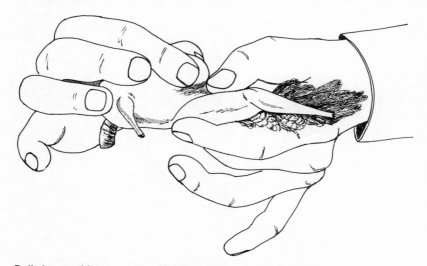

Pull the quail breast up and back to open the body cavity.

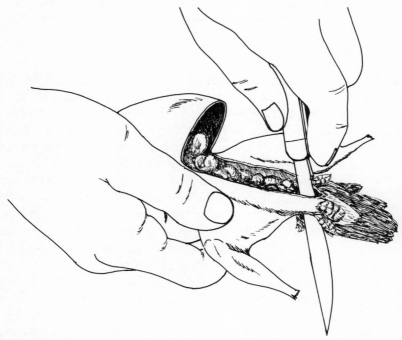

With a sharp knife, slice along each side of the vent.

Cut off vent and
remove entrails at
the same time

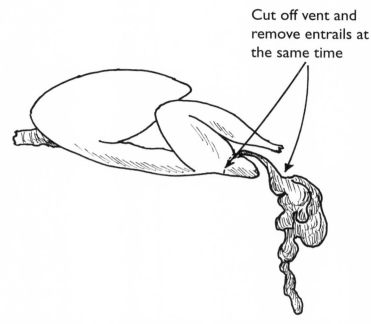

Pull the quail entrails out of the cavity. Cut off the tail and vent with
the entrails attached.

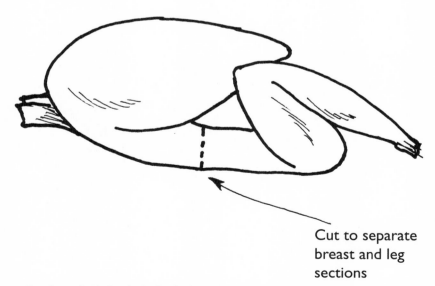

Cut to separate
breast and leg
sections

Quail can be left whole for baking or cut up for frying. One method is to
cut the legs off in one section, leaving the breast.

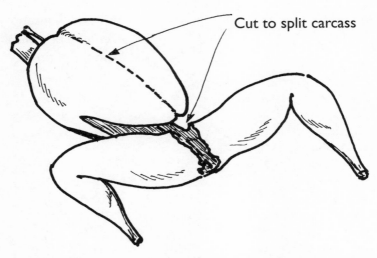

You can also split the carcass with game shears, providing a half-bird for easier frying or grilling.

Quail for frying or grilling can also be split down the back and breast into two half sections with a pair of game shears. Do this after skinning and removing the head, wings, and legs, as above.

Split the breast first.

Then turn over and split down the backbone.

Some hunters prefer to pluck upland game birds rather than skin them, but this must be done as quickly as possible, preferably in the field, before the feathers "set."

DOVES

Doves can be skinned in the same manner as quail, although they're more often "breasted," with the breast removed from the carcass. Breasting doves is quick and easy. Insert your fingertips into the soft spot below the breastbone and bend upward. A pair of game shears can be used to clip the breast from the wing bones and backbone, or you can simply snap the breast free. A small patch of skin will come off with the breast, and you can simply pull this off and discard.

Dove feathers stick to your hands like glue, and the best tactic is to breast all the birds you have collected and place them in a clean spot. Then pull off the skin and remaining feathers and place the breasts in a pan of water. Pour off any feathers that float on the water and wash the feathers and blood off your hands. The feathers will easily come off your hands and the breasts in that manner; if you breast and wash each piece separately, however, you'll have

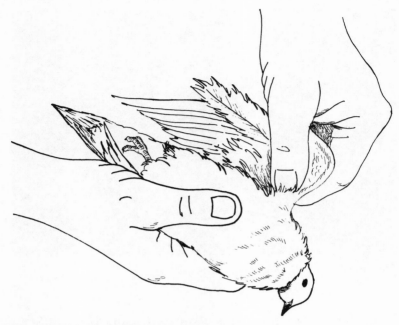

Doves are quite often breasted. Twist off the wings.

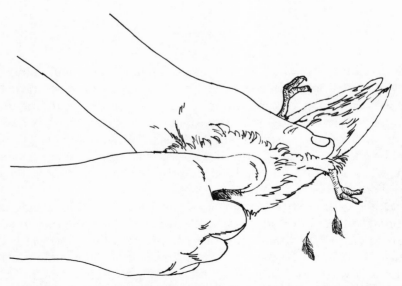

Insert the tips of your fingers into the soft spot below the breastbone and bend the breast upward until you can snap it free.

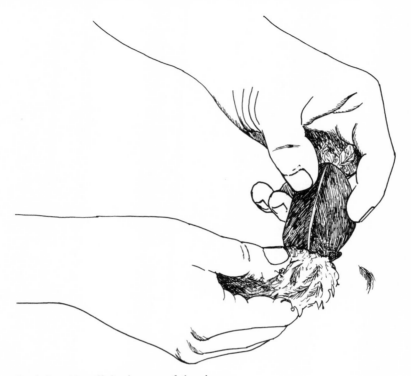

Peel the skin off the breast of the dove.

feathers everywhere. If hunting with friends, create an assembly line, in which one friend can do one chore and another a different step in the cleaning process.

GROUSE AND PHEASANTS

Larger birds, such as grouse and pheasants, can either be plucked or skinned in the same manner as quail. If the birds are to be cooked whole, such as baked, you may wish to pluck them. A number of years ago, a friend went along on an Idaho elk hunt only to fish and cook while the rest of us hunted big game. He thoroughly enjoyed popping "fool's hen" grouse near camp, dry plucked the birds as soon as he shot them, and baked them in a Dutch oven. That was some of the best camp food I've ever experienced.

Pheasants, grouse, and other larger upland birds can be skinned or plucked. If plucking, do it as soon as possible.

Game birds can be dry plucked, then the down and pinfeathers singed off with a match, lighter, or butane torch. If dry plucking, do it as soon as possible, because the feathers can set within minutes, making them difficult to remove without tearing the skin. You can also scald the birds for easier plucking (see Chapter 4 for more information on scalding birds).

If you prefer to skin pheasants or grouse, grasp the feathers on the breast and pull up toward the head to start the skinning process. On tougher birds, you may wish to first make a slit with a sharp knife along the breastbone. Peel the skin down to the inside of the legs and up to the neck, then continue to peel the skin away from the rest of the carcass. Skinning the back is the hardest and may require some judicious cuts with the knife to release the skin. Continue peeling the skin off the neck, then cut off the head and remove the crop. Pull the skin out to the last joint of the wings, and cut off the wings at that joint. Peel the skin down over the thighs to the legs. Bend back the legs at the joint, and cut them off with a sharp knife. Pull the skin down to the tail, and cut off the tail at the base.

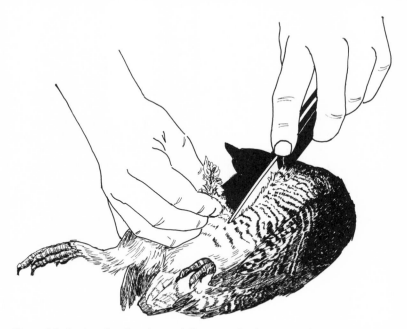

Game birds can also be skinned. Start at the breast and, using your fingers or a sharp knife, make a beginning tear or cut.

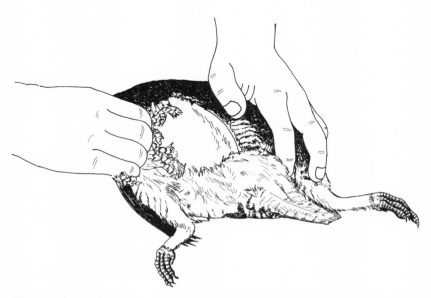

Then peel the skin down one side of the breast to a leg. Repeat for the opposite side.

Peel the skin away from the thighs and legs. Then turn the bird and pull the skin from the back and sides. This will normally come off in two pieces: the upper and lower sections.

Remove the head and crop.

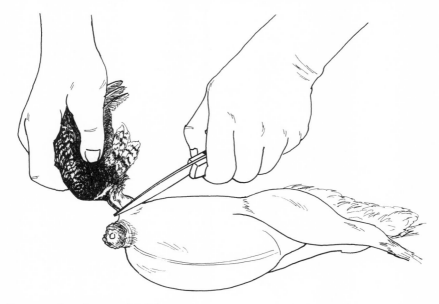

Remove the wings at the joint.

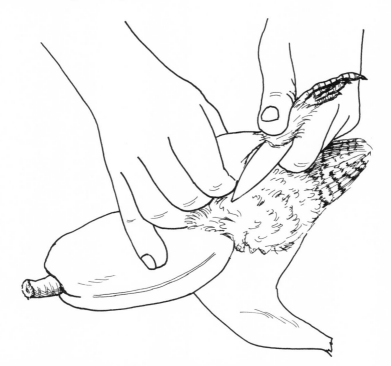

Bend the legs at the joint and cut off the lower portions.

Once the bird has been plucked or skinned, cut off the head, re-move the crop, then make an incision across the soft skin below the breastbone. Bend the breastbone back until you can reach in and pull out the entrails. Pull entrails down toward the tailpiece, then make a 45-degree cut on each side of the tailpiece to remove the tailpiece, vent, and entrails all in one section.

Although birds dressed in this manner are excellent cooked whole in a covered dish or by baking, they're more often cut into smaller pieces for baking or frying or, in the case of old birds, for cooking in a slow cooker.

The birds may also be quartered, with the pieces usually consist-ing of the breast unit, two legs, and two wings. The first step in cut-ting up the bird is to grasp a wing and pull it out from the body, then cut through the joint with a sharp knife. Next spread the legs to pop or dislocate the hip joint. Cut through the dislocated joint to remove the legs and thigh pieces. The final step is to pull the breast up and forward, cut through the ribs to both sides of the backbone, then cut

Make an incision below the breastbone and bend it back.

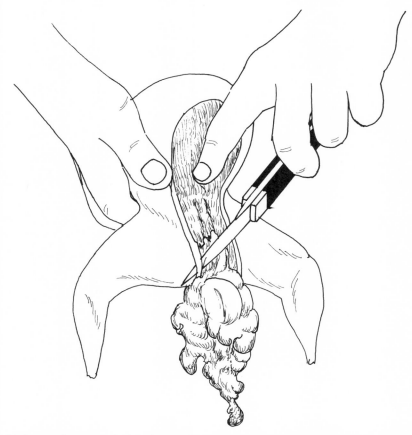

Pull out the entrails but leave them attached to the vent. Make a 45-degree cut on each side of the tailpiece, then remove tailpiece and entrails all in one section.

through the shoulder meat near the neck and peel the breast away. You can discard the backbone or, if you're dressing several birds, place the backbones in a stew pot for some excellent soup stock.

Livers, hearts, and gizzards are a favorite with many hunters and can be collected as the entrails are removed, except while field dressing in hot weather. If you're keeping the liver, make sure you cut it away from the bile sack.

Game birds such as pheasants or grouse can also be breasted. In this case, rather than popping out the entire breast, including the breastbone (such as when dressing doves), the breast is filleted by removing the meat from each side of the breastbone. This is an ex-

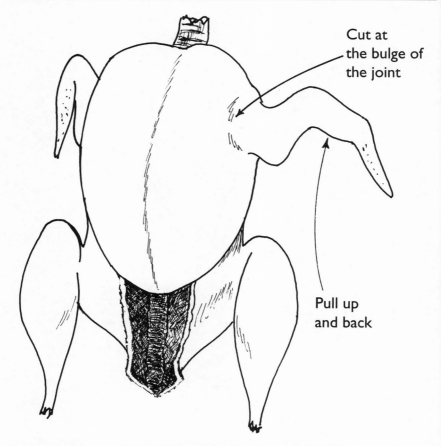

Cut at
the bulge of
the joint

Pull up
and back

Larger game birds can be kept whole or quartered. With the bird on a flat surface, pull a wing up and back to reveal the rounded joint inside the muscle. Cut through the muscle at the joint. Repeat for the opposite wing.

cellent method of dressing the older birds for baked dishes and casseroles. The bird can be breasted without skinning, or the bird can be skinned, the breast removed, and the legs, thighs, and wings used in soup stock or other recipes. To breast, lay the bird on its back with the tail pointing toward you. Pinch a bit of skin and feathers just over the breast and tear the skin away from the breast meat to expose the breast. Then remove the breast meat by using a fillet knife to cut around the ribs and debone the breast.

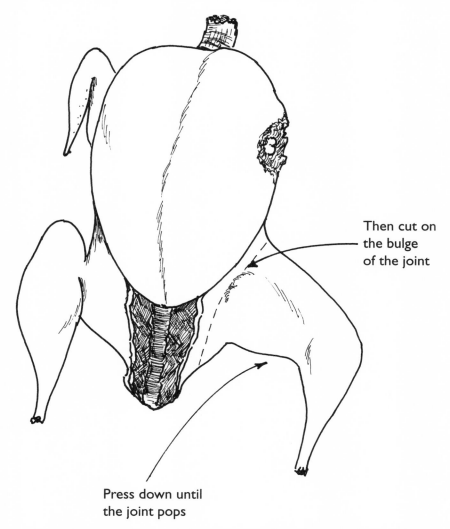

Then cut on
the bulge
of the joint

Press down until
the joint pops

Press down on a leg until the joint pops free, then cut the muscle surrounding the joint. Repeat for the opposite leg.

GAME BIRD TROPHY CARE

Most game birds make beautiful trophy mounts, especially pheasants, quail, and grouse. Proper field care of the birds will assure a quality mount. Do not dress or eviscerate the bird if you plan to

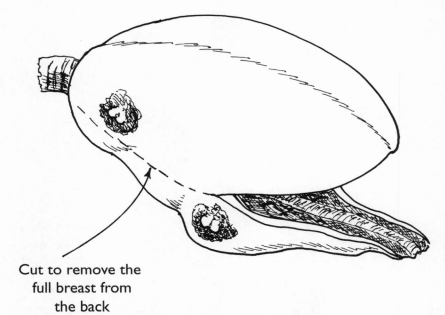

Cut to remove the
full breast from
the back

Pull the breastbone upward and cut through the ribs on both sides to remove the in-bone whole breast.

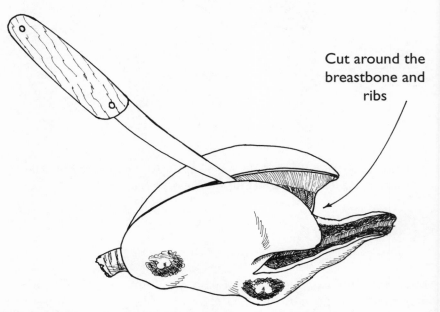

Cut around the
breastbone and
ribs

You can also bone out the breast meat using a boning knife.

If you intend to have a bird mounted, such as this trophy, don't eviscerate it, but carefully wipe away all blood while still in the field, and make sure feathers don't get ruffled.

have it mounted. Carry a soft cloth in your vest to wipe off any blood as soon as you pick up the bird in the field. Wipe with the direction of the feathers, taking care not to ruffle them. If the blood

Roll the bird in newspaper and place in a cooler until it can be frozen or taken to the taxidermist.

doesn't wipe off easily, dampen the cloth. Stuff tissue into the nostrils and mouth to stop bleeding in those areas.

Next, roll the bird in a section of clean newspaper or place it in a paper bag. Carry the bird head down or place it flat on a smooth surface in your automobile for transporting. Do not put the bird in a plastic bag for transporting home, but do keep it in a cool spot. A cooler with ice can be used, but the bird should not be allowed to soak in melting ice water; rather, it should be held above the ice. Long tail feathers must not be bent.

Once you have the bird home, examine it carefully to make sure that no blood has seeped onto the feathers. Straighten and smooth out any feathers that may be ruffled. A pheasant with a long tail is the hardest to maintain. I use large cardboard shipping tubes to hold pheasants in the freezer and prevent tail damage. First I wrap the pheasant body in freezer paper and tie around the feet and tail without compressing the tail. Then I lower the bird headfirst into the tube and apply duct tape on each end of the tube to close it off. This practically guarantees that the bird will stay intact. Keep the bird frozen until you can deliver it to the taxidermist, and don't thaw the bird before you deliver it.

CHAPTER

3

Dressing Waterfowl

lthough it's not quite pitch dark, dawn is still a bit away. We're in the decoys, untangling lines, tossing blocks into a semblance of a flock of ducks, whispering among ourselves, the excitement of opening day growing with each moment. There's a sudden flurry of wings as a half-dozen green-wing teal try to sit down among us. We anxiously speed up our efforts. Finally, the last decoy is out and we scurry to the makeshift blind. We look at our watches again, and again, and again. There are still minutes until shooting time, and four more batches of teal have dropped into our decoys, nonchalantly swimming among their silent brethren. Then a half-dozen widgeon drop in as well, and the waiting gets tougher.

"Mallards at 4:00," my son Mark whispers tensely. "What time is it?"

"Shooting time," declares Scrappy, glancing at his watch and the shooting time chart in his hand.

"Now what?" whispers Harold, sitting next to Scrappy. "Do we take the ducks we have in hand, or try for the mallards?"

Mark doesn't answer; he's already on his call, giving coaxing sit-down calls to the dozen or so mallards that have disappeared behind our blind. We hear the quack of the lead hen, and a few soft quacks answer from our decoy set. Mark wisely shuts up and the mallards make a swing in front of the blind, just past our last decoy and out of range, then disappear again behind the blind. It's so still the blind and its inhabitants, including Mark's Chessie, could be statues. Even though this is a long way from my first duck season opener, I can feel my heart begin to pound in anticipation.

"TAKE 'EM!" Mark exclaims, and we jump to our feet. In front of us is absolute pandemonium. The flock of mallards seems to hang for a second right in front of the blind, big red feet and legs waving

Waterfowl range from tiny teal to giant Canada geese and have been a mainstay food from the beginning of mankind.

Some hunters like to hang wildfowl, especially waterfowl, for a day or two to let the carcasses age.

absurdly as they always do on descent. Then the flock turns in an instant, wings beating desperately for altitude. The ducks in the decoys are also scrambling, the teal springing upward in a spray of water and the widgeon coming off the water as though jet propelled. It's a mass of ducks flying in every direction, the noise of the shotgun barrage lost in the confusion.

Suddenly it's quiet, with smoke clearing and feathers and ducks drifting on the rippling water. "Only six ducks from four hunters," Mark laments. "Boy, we're lousy! Guess it was kind of a confusing opener, but man that was fun!"

Waterfowl provide not only some of the most mysterious, glamorous, and exciting hunting, but table fare fit for any occasion if dressed to match the cooking method and cared for properly.

When it comes to waterfowl, many like to hunt them, most enjoy eating them, but few like to clean them. The reason is that they're one of the hardest birds to dress. Four dressing methods can be used: dry plucking, wax plucking, skinning, and breasting. The cooking method, age, and species dictate how the bird should be dressed. If waterfowl are to be baked or smoked, they should be plucked, leaving as much of the skin intact as possible to retain the natural juices while cooking.

Some people like to hang waterfowl for a few days, though my son Mark hangs his for a week. This works if the weather stays between 35 and 45°F. If the weather is colder, the birds freeze; warmer, and they spoil. I often hunt several days per week, and instead of dressing birds each time I come home, I simply place them in an old refrigerator and leave them until the week is over. If I'm not planning on hunting for a few days, or if I have a big batch of birds, then I dress the birds all at once.

Regardless of the hanging or aging method used, it's a good idea to eviscerate the bird first. Make a cut across the bird directly below the breastbone, and remove the entrails through the opening.

Dry Plucking

Dry plucking is the most tedious and time-consuming method of dressing waterfowl, but also the most convenient. The key is to pluck the bird as soon as possible, while it's still warm and before the feathers have set. One old-timer I hunted with years ago sat in

Dry plucking is a common method of cleaning waterfowl, regardless of the species, but it can be tedious. Start at the top of the breast and work downward, then pluck sides and back.

the blind and dry plucked his birds while waiting for the next flight. The feathers and down went into a paper bag, and a small cooler held the finished carcasses. It was an extremely effective method of whiling away "bluebird" hours. It is important, however, to leave the sex and species identification in the way of wings, head, and feet. Check with your game and fish department for specific rules and regulations.

To pluck waterfowl, hold the bird over a paper sack, start at the top of the breast, and dry pick downward. Once you have finished plucking the breast, pluck the sides and the back. Larger, heavier birds such as geese are best plucked on a table; if you have several to do, place them on a box between your legs and sit in a chair. Geese are also plucked downward. It does take some effort to dry pluck a goose, but the results in the pot are well worth it. You may wish to remove the wing ends first to keep them out of the way for plucking.

If you pluck a number of waterfowl each season, a mechanical plucker may be a good idea. These use rubber fingers on a rotating drum to quickly and easily remove feathers and down.

Small pinfeathers will be left on the carcass regardless of whether you hand pluck or use a mechanical plucker. You can pull these out by grasping them with your finger and the side of a sharp knife, or by using tweezers. A number of other fine feathers and hairs will remain, and these are best singed off with a butane torch.

Wax Plucking

Wax makes the chore of plucking easier. Melt paraffin wax in a double-boiler arrangement, such as a large pan inside a larger pan containing water. *Do not allow flames to contact the wax or wax container,* as the wax is extremely flammable. Use only enough heat to melt the wax and keep it in a liquid state, not boiling. Beeswax can be added to the paraffin to help hold the wax together. You'll need about 4 to 5 pounds of paraffin for a session. While waiting for the wax to heat, remove the wings from the birds. This will allow you to coat all the feathers around the sides with wax. To remove the wing, twist backward and cut at the joint where it joins the body. Cut first through the muscle, then continue to twist until you can locate and cut at the ball and socket joint. You can also remove the feet if you desire, bending back the legs and cutting off at the joint. The head should be left as a handhold for dipping. You can also rough pluck some of the feathers before dipping.

Once the wax is melted, dip the bird into the hot wax, legs first, holding it by the head. Use an old kitchen ladle or wooden stick to push the carcass down in the wax. Remove and place the bird on a newspaper to allow the wax to cool and harden. This only takes a few minutes. If you have several birds to do, dip them all, placing them on newspapers to cool as you dip. Dip the birds at least twice—or more as needed—to acquire a solid coating of wax over the feathers and down. Once all the birds have been thoroughly coated and have hardened, grasp a handful of wax and feathers and pull them off in one smooth motion. Repeat this until the majority of the feathers have been removed. Redip as necessary. Some small down and feathers will still need to be singed off with a butane torch.

As you peel off the wax and feathers, place them in an old pot. When the pot is full, heat the wax until it liquefies, skim off the larger feathers with an old kitchen skimmer, then pour the hot wax

Wax plucking is easier. The first step is to melt paraffin wax in a double boiler, such as a pan inside a larger pan containing water. Do not allow the flame to contact wax or wax residue.

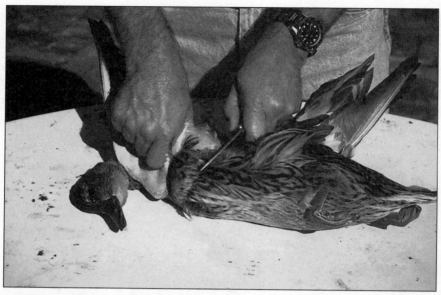

Remove the wings, as this allows the wax to thoroughly coat the body. Twist wing back and up, and cut through muscle and tissue of joint.

Dip bird in the hot wax, legs first. Push bird down in wax.

Place on a clean surface for wax to cool and harden. Dip again if necessary.

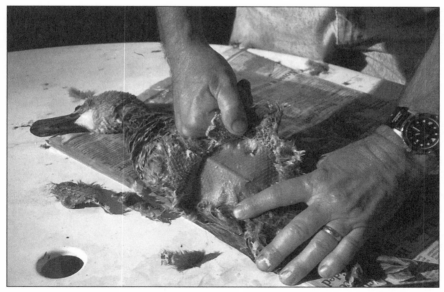

Grasp a handful of wax and feathers and pull off. Most will come off in sheets.

Singe off small down and feathers with a propane torch.

Remove the head.

Remove the feet and tail.

and small feathers through a piece of hardware cloth back into another container and allow it to cool. The wax is now ready for use with more birds.

Once the bird has been plucked, use a sharp knife to remove the head and eviscerate the bird. To remove the entrails, make a

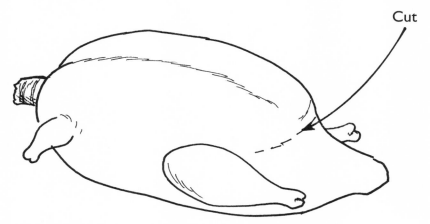

Eviscerate by cutting through belly skin and removing entrails.

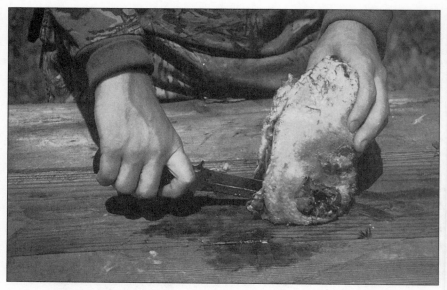

Removing the backbone makes it easier to cook whole ducks. It also makes it easier to eviscerate. Stand bird up on its neck bone and cut down from base of tail through ribs to neck. Repeat for the opposite side.

Pull out the backbone and neck, and the entrails come with it.

slicing cut across the belly muscle but not into the entrails. Pinching up the muscle will help alleviate the problem of cutting too deeply. Grasp the breastbone, pull back, then continue the cut down both sides of the flank to open the bird. Reach in and extract the entrails, pulling them down toward the tail, then cut off the tail.

Another way to dress waterfowl is to remove the backbone. This makes eviscerating easy and also makes it easier to prepare and cook the whole bird. To remove the backbone, stand the bird up on its neck bone and cut from the base of the tail downward on each side of the backbone through the ribs and down the side of the neck. When you remove the backbone and neck, the entrails come free as well.

Once the bird has been plucked and eviscerated, wash it well, pick out any shot, and cut away any bloody areas. Place it in a pan of salt water overnight in the refrigerator, as this will help to draw out any remaining blood.

Tip: If you have several waterfowl to do, pluck all of them, then remove the heads, wings, and eviscerate them. This will keep your hands clean and free of blood during the plucking operation and, once all have been eviscerated, you can then do a cleanup session.

SKINNING

Ducks and geese are often diced and added to dishes such as gumbo, baked in exotic wine sauces, or ground into sausage. In this case, it's not necessary to spend the time plucking the bird, as the skin is removed before cooking anyway. Waterfowl, like most game birds, can be easily skinned. Simply slit along the breastbone and then peel off the skin. One patch of skin sticks like glue to each side of the breast, and the back skin is also fairly tough to remove. Skinning can wait until you get home, as it doesn't matter as much whether the bird is freshly skinned or skinned later. The skin does, however, release easier the quicker it's done after the bird is killed.

Small ducks can be skinned in the same manner as previously described for larger game birds. Geese and larger ducks are best skinned in the following manner: Before skinning, remove the feet and wings, and hang the bird by the neck. Starting at the top of the breast, make a cut around the neck skin, then pull the skin downward over the breast. Use a knife to loosen the skin as needed. The

Pull the skin back down each side of the breast, then continue skinning around legs, thighs, and back.

skin will easily come off on the breast and sides, but it is anchored tightly in the middle of the back. Once skinned, and if not already done, make a cut below the breastbone and eviscerate the bird, or, better yet, remove the backbone and eviscerate as described earlier.

BREASTING

Pan-fried duck breast is a delicacy much favored at our house. If you intend to use waterfowl for that purpose, they can simply be breasted. Waterfowl breasting is the removal of the breast meat, producing two fillets and discarding the remainder of the carcass. This is an extremely fast and effective method when you have a fairly large take of small ducks, such as bluebills or scaup. Ducks that are pretty well shot up are also good choices for breasting. Teal, on the other hand, are absolutely the best for dry plucking and cooking whole.

Generous goose populations and limits, especially of snows and blues in some areas, can often produce an awesome plucking chore

Larger birds, such as Canada geese, are best skinned by first hanging by the neck. Then cut around the neck skin and peel the skin down over the breast to start the skinning process.

these days. Check over the birds. Those that do not have fat on them, or that appear to be lean, will tend to be tougher roasted and are prime subjects for breasting. A prime, young Canada goose, however, should be kept back for Christmas dinner and roasted with all the trimmings.

Regardless of duck or goose, the breasting method is the same. You'll need a sharp boning or fillet knife. My favorite is a butcher's boning knife. It's big enough to handle easily, but the blade bends and follows the bone. The first step in breasting is to feel for the sharp center edge of the breastbone with your fingers. Make a light cut just through the skin at this point. Place the first two fingers of each hand inside the opening and pull the skin apart in both directions to completely expose the breast meat. Insert the point of the knife at the top center in the approximate location of the center of the Y-bone and along one side of the center of the breastbone. Slice downward along the center of the breastbone. Use the blade to follow the breastbone and ribs sideways, and cut away the breast, pulling it away with the opposite hand.

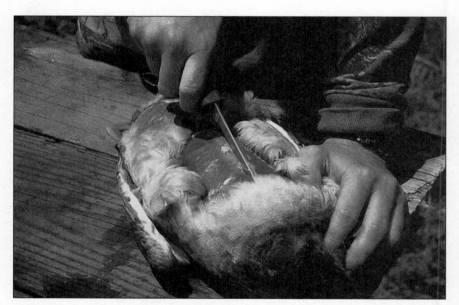

To breast waterfowl, make a cut to one side of the breastbone just through the skin. Place two fingers inside each side of the cut, and pull the skin back away from both sides of the breast, down to the thighs, and up to the wings.

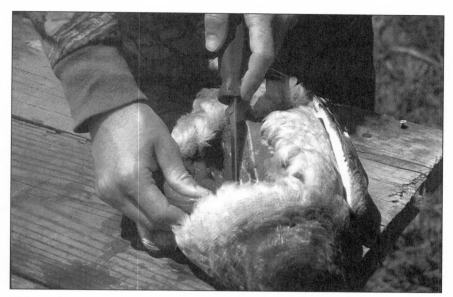

Make a cut down the side of the breastbone with a sharp boning knife.

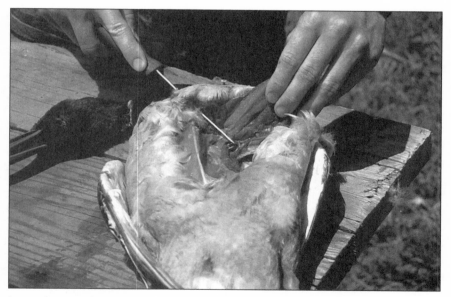

Insert fingers of opposite hand inside cut and push breast meat away as you continue cutting along the backbone and around the rib cage until the breast fillet comes away.

At this point, all but the upper portion of the breast at the wing joint should be loose. Turn the knife, and starting at the beginning of your first cut, slice upward, following the Y-bone to the wing. Then cut through the tough muscle joining the wing to the breast and lift free. Repeat for the other breast. With a little practice, the chore can be done in a couple of minutes, and you'll have a clean, boneless breast piece ready to slice and fry or bake.

You can also remove the entire breast on smaller waterfowl, such as scaup or other divers that don't pan fry as well. First, peel the skin from the breast. Then insert the fingers of one hand into the opening cut made during field dressing and pull up and back- ward. At the same time, insert the fingers of your opposite hand and hold down firmly on the back. With a little effort, the breast will "pop" back away from the rest of the carcass. Using the point of a knife, cut the wings away from the breast at the wing joint. Con- tinue cutting through the muscles around the wing, cut through the joint of the Y-bone at each wing, and pull back on the breast until it can be freed with the skin and muscles around the neck. You end up with a nice bone-in breast ready for baking.

Dressing Wild Turkey

W ell before daylight, you begin the ascent up the old log-ging road to the top of the ridge, slowly picking your way in the darkness. Panting from exertion, you reach the ridge top just as fingers of gray dawn begin to reach through the freshly leaved hardwoods. After a moment's rest against a huge white oak, you cup your hands to your mouth and roll out a barred owl call, smiling as it echoes up and down the undulating ridges. The sound barely stops ringing before you hear a gobble, far across on the opposite mountaintop. Then you hear another, farther away on the same distant mountain. Then a third, possibly a bit closer. You roll out another owl call and the distant gobbles are repeated, but no sounds come from the ridge you've spent the past 30 min-utes climbing. You shrug your shoulders and begin to move down the mountainside at a rapid clip. You have to cover a great deal of vertical landscape in a short amount of time if you want to collect one of the old gobblers still ringing forth their challenge to the early spring morning.

An hour later, you're sitting on a mountainside bench, leaning against a red oak, and your heart is pounding with excitement. Two gobblers are also on this bench, 100 yards or so away, and gobbling at every call you make. Their calls at times seem closer, at times more distant. You've been working the birds for almost half an hour. Finally, you roll over onto your side, then belly crawl 50 yards away from the birds. You get into position, give a soft yelp, and scratch the leaves with your hand. A booming gobble responds im-mediately. You sit quietly, as patiently as possible, gun up on your knees and hopeful. Suddenly you spot movement, and a dark form materializes behind a screen of young oaks. You spot the white head, red wattles, and beard of a gobbler. Slowly you move the

Wild turkeys, the American wildlife success story, not only provide big-game excitement to hunters across the nation, but some of the finest eating.

muzzle toward the form, click off the safety, and wait. "Just another few steps," you think. The gobbler hesitates, looking for the hen he just heard. He takes a slow step forward, then another. The bead of the shotgun is centered just below his wattles, and the gun goes off almost without you knowing it. Within minutes you're examining one of America's greatest trophies, a mature wild turkey gobbler. As you heft the bird to roll him over onto your shoulder, you groan at the 20-pound-plus weight. It won't be easy packing him out, but then, you have plenty of time. Plus, the morel mushrooms are out, so you can rest and hunt morels along the trickling stream in the cleft of the valley below as you head back to your car.

Just as wild turkey hunting can provide some of the most exciting outdoor moments, the meat of the wild turkey can provide some of the most delicious meals. Like other wildfowl, wild turkeys can also be plucked, skinned, or breasted, depending on how the bird is to be cooked and the age of the bird. Younger birds can be fried, deep fried, roasted, baked, or smoked. Older birds are best breasted and baked, slow cooked, or smoked, with the legs and thighs going into a slow cooker for soups or stews.

AGING YOUR WILD TURKEY

The first step is to determine the age of your bird. Many myths surround this subject. Some say that any bird heavier than 20 pounds is at least 3 years old. Others say that a 9-inch beard is a sure sign that your turkey is at least 4 years old. Still others claim that a sharp spur that is at least ¾ inch long indicates a 3-year-old bird.

The National Wild Turkey Federation provides some information that would seem to settle much of the debate about a turkey's age. Many things can affect the weight of a bird, so weight is not a factor. Spur and beard length, however, are important factors in determining age. The federation provides the following rules of thumb:

Spur Length	Age of Turkey
½ inch or less	1 year
½ to ⅞ inch	2 years
⅞ to 1 inch	3 years
1+ inches	4+ years

Beard Length	Age of Turkey
3 to 5 inches	1 year
6 to 9 inches	2 years
10+ inches	3+ years

To differentiate juvenile and adult birds from a distance, look at the tail fan. A bird with longer feathers in the middle of the fan is a juvenile, whereas a uniform length in tail feathers indicates an adult bird. With a harvested bird, you can distinguish the adult bird from

Aging birds, especially wild turkey, is important to determine the type of preparation and cooking needed. Shown is a juvenile jake turkey.

In hot weather you need to draw the bird and cool it as quickly as possible in a large cooler. Placing ice bags inside the body cavity can help speed the cooling.

the juvenile by examining the two outermost primary wing feathers—those longest feathers on the end of the wing. On adult birds, these two primaries will be rounded and have white barring extending to the very end. On juvenile birds, these feathers will be much more pointed and have no barring near the tip.

In hot weather, you may wish to eviscerate the bird in the field. Do this by making a cut just above the vent and removing the entrails. (Check local game laws regarding this, as some states require birds to be checked at a check station whole.) A large cooler can also be used to keep the bird cool while transporting to the check station. Coleman makes the 50-quart Xtreme Wheeled Cooler that will transport even a record bird. Some hunters like to insert a small bag of ice or even a can of cold soda into the cavity.

PLUCKING

Dry plucking a young bird is fairly easy, whereas dry plucking an old bird just the opposite—very tough. The back feathers in particu-

Young turkeys can be dry plucked.

lar can be extremely hard to pull out. Plucking as soon as possible after recovering the bird makes the chore somewhat easier.

Water plucking, or scalding, is the easiest. It's the same method used for years by farmers to pluck domestic fowl. Do this chore outside. You'll need something big enough to hold the entire bird. My friend and long-time turkey hunting companion, Jerry Thies, scalds turkey in a big cooler and says it holds the heat better than any pot. Heat water in a pot over a fish-fryer base, camp stove, or fire until the water is boiling. Once it is boiling, pour it into the cooler. You may have to heat more than one pot of water to have enough water to scald a big turkey.

While waiting for the water to boil, grasp the beard at the juncture next to the skin and pull it off. Cut off and remove the fan and vent. You can also make the scalding chore easier by cutting off the wings at the first joint. Although some cooks like to keep the entire wing intact, this is more for appearance than food volume. Do not eviscerate a bird that is going to be scalded.

Once the water is boiling, grasp the turkey by the neck and dip it down into the water. Use a stick to help push the bird down as far

Water plucking or scalding is best. Use a cooler or plastic bucket to hold heated water.

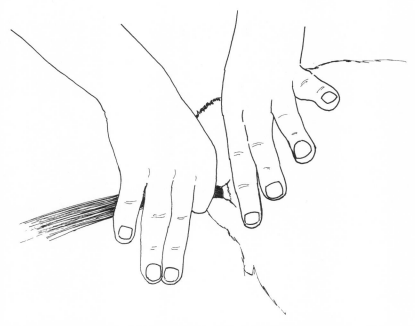

Remove the beard by grasping at the base and pulling away from skin.

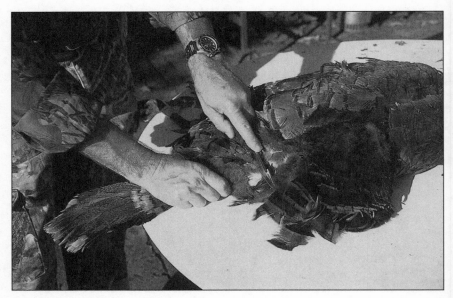

Cut off fan and vent.

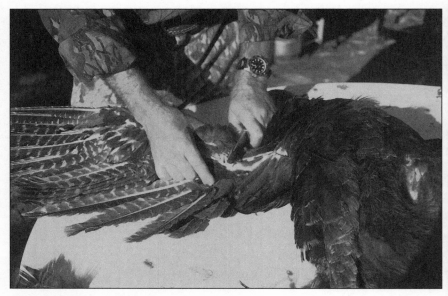

Cut off wings at wing socket.

Cut off the legs at the joints. Bend back at the joint to find cut location.

as possible. Leave the turkey in the water at least a full minute. Remove the bird, try a few feathers, then dip again if the feathers don't release easily. Start with the wing and tail feathers, picking them out first. Continue with the larger quill feathers, then do the back, and finally the breast. The breast feathers come out the easiest. If you can't dip the entire bird at one time, turn the carcass over, dip the second half, and pluck in the same manner.

With the bird plucked, bend back the legs at the knee joint and cut off the legs. A bit of skin will remain at the leg joint. Cut and pull this away to reveal the clean joint. Cut off the neck and head. Pull out the crop. Eviscerate the bird and wash the entire carcass inside and out.

Livers, hearts, and gizzards are favored by many hunters, especially for the Thanksgiving turkey. These giblets can be collected as the entrails are removed, except when field dressing birds in hot weather. Carefully cut the liver away from the bile sack, and cut open and clean the gizzard.

Grasp the bird by the neck and dip in scalding water. Use a stick to push the legs and tail end down in the water. Leave for about a minute.

Remove and lay on a clean surface until the feathers cool enough to pull them out.

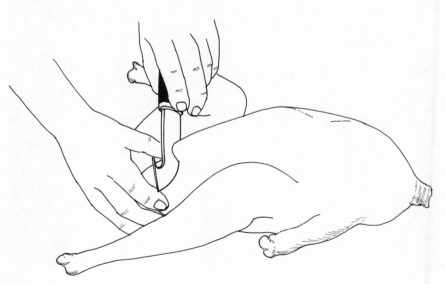

Cut off the head. Eviscerate by making a cut across the belly skin. Reach in and pull windpipe, lungs, and all entrails out. Save liver and gizzard for Thanksgiving gravy.

SKINNING

Wild turkeys can also be skinned fairly easily, and these birds can be cooked by smoking or baking. Lay the bird flat on a table, or hang by the neck, and use a sharp knife to make a slit along the

Wild turkeys can also be skinned, and it's best to hang them by the neck at a convenient working level.

breastbone. Pull the skin back from the breastbone on both sides. Then pull the skin down around a leg until you reach the joint. Bend the joint back, and cut off the leg. Repeat for the opposite leg. Pull the skin away from the back in two pieces, one toward the tail and one toward the head. Pull the lower section down to the tail, and cut off the tail along with the fan. Pull the upper section up to the wings and cut off the wing by bending it back to reveal the muscle and joint. Cut through at the joint to the body. Continue to peel the skin over the shoulders up to the neck, then cut off the neck and head. Eviscerate the bird and rinse the carcass.

BREASTING

Wild turkeys can also be breasted, which is a good method if you're flying on an out-of-state hunting trip and have little room to take home a large cooler of meat. Breasting is also a good method for an older bird. To breast, position the bird on its back with the feet toward you. Slice through the skin along one side of the breastbone, and pull the skin away from the breast. Pull the skin down over the

To breast, slit skin and peel back from breast. Use boning knife to slice along breastbone and down along rib cage.

leg and around to the back, as well as down around the wing area to reveal the entire breast. Slice along the breastbone down one side to the ribs. Then turn the knife sideways and slice along the rib cage up to meet the first cut. Start at the rear of the breast, and work toward the wing. Slice around the Y-bone, and pull the breast back to reveal the muscle joining it at the wing. Cut through this muscle. Repeat the steps for the opposite breast.

You can discard the rest of the turkey, or skin out the legs and thighs and save them for specific recipes, such as gumbo.

CHAPTER 5

Freezing Wildfowl

The steps to quality game-bird meat don't stop with the field-dressing and butchering processes. Proper storage is just as important. Although several methods can be used to preserve meat, the most common method is freezing. Although simple and effective, there are limits to freezing's ability to maintain quality. Freezing protects from immediate spoilage but affects quality and flavor by drying out the meat. This is especially true in frost-free freezers, where moisture is pulled from the refrigerated air to prevent frost buildup.

It is important to handle meat correctly before wrapping it. Remove all fat from game birds, because fat can often turn rancid, even while frozen. Freeze boneless breast meat intact rather than sliced ready to fry. Moisture escapes from each cut surface, speeding deterioration. Cut the meat as desired after it has partially thawed but is still firm enough to slice easily.

WRAPPING FOWL

Wrap the meat carefully to maintain quality for as long as possible. Heavy-duty freezer paper or aluminum foil can be used. They are equally effective, although foil is easier to use on odd-shaped pieces. Plastic zippered freezer bags are very convenient for freezing small game birds or breasted waterfowl. Double wrapping is a better method, however. First use plastic food wrap, then follow with freezer paper, aluminum foil, or a zippered bag. If you're using freezer paper, use freezer tape to seal the package.

Make certain you mark the packages as to the contents and the month and year. You might also want to note the specific trip, such as South Dakota pheasants and trip date. Jotting down everything on a separate list can also help you keep things organized and ensures that you'll consume the older packages first. Regardless of how careful we are about labeling, though, it seems that once or twice a year we pull out a mystery package with no label. What I thought was quail turned out to be dove. This can cause a problem when you were planning to fry quail for guests.

When wrapping meat, squeeze as much air from the package as possible. When small pieces are to be frozen together, such as quail or small breast pieces, air is best eliminated by using water packing. Using plastic bags or containers, stack the meat pieces, cover them with water, then freeze. Once frozen, add more water if necessary. Water-packed meat will generally last longer than standard butcher-wrapped meat.

Another method of water freezing is to glaze coat the individual pieces of meat and freeze them on open trays. Lay pieces of meat on a plastic-wrap-covered tray, mist spray the top surface with water, then freeze. Mist spray all surfaces of the meat with two coats of water, freezing between coats and before packaging. This will keep the meat pieces separate while frozen, much like the large bags of chicken breasts available in the super market. This also gives some extra freezer-burn protection.

Storage Times

You should plan to use all game within a year of freezing. Not only does this provide the best meat, but it is often necessary to follow some game laws regarding possession. Be sure to check with your state regarding game possession regulations, including what you may have stored in your freezer. Depending on how the meat is wrapped and what type of freezer is used, quality may remain constant for longer periods. Freezing for longer periods affects taste and quality but poses no other risks. The following chart gives an approximate storage guide for various cuts of meat.

Meat type	Maximum storage
Waterfowl, butcher wrap	8 months
Waterfowl, water pack	12 months
Small birds, cut in pieces, butcher wrap	8 months
Whole large birds, butcher wrap	5 months
Whole small birds, butcher wrap	6 months
Whole small birds, water pack	1 year
Large turkey breast, butcher wrap	10 months

Vacuum Packing

The ultimate method of preserving by freezing is using a vacuum-packing machine to remove oxygen from the container. Oxidation (exposure to oxygen in the air) is the main cause of food spoilage. When foods absorb oxygen, they begin a process of irreversible chemical change. Contact with oxygen causes foods to lose nutritional value, texture, flavor, and overall quality.

When oxygen is removed from the storage environment, foods can be stored three to five times longer than with conventional storage methods. In the absence of oxygen, dried, frozen, and perishable foods requiring refrigeration will retain their freshness and flavor much longer—resulting in less food waste.

Oxygen enables microorganisms such as bacteria, mold, and yeast to grow. These microorganisms cause rapid deterioration of food. Exposure to freezing-cold air also causes freezer burn in frozen foods. (Freezer burn is localized dehydration.) Oxygen causes foods that are moderately high in fats and oils to yield a rancid odor and flavor. Air carries moisture, and moisture causes the food to become soggy and lose its texture. Moisture causes caking in dry solids, making them difficult to handle. Oxygen also allows insects to survive and hatch.

Preventing air from coming in contact with stored food is a two-step process:

Step 1. Remove all the air currently in the container.
Step 2. Prevent air from reentering the container.

This requires that two conditions be met:

1. The container needs to be made of a material that provides a barrier to oxygen.
2. The seal on the container needs to be airtight.

Vacuum packaging is the process of removing the air from a container so that a vacuum is created, and then sealing the container so that air cannot reenter.

Vacuum-packaging systems are able to create a vacuum in storage bags, canisters, jars, cans, and bottles. Storage bags used for freezing are specially designed to provide an oxygen and moisture barrier and to maintain an airtight seal. To provide an effective barrier, the bags should be constructed of plastic or a nylon layer. The

The ultimate in freezing longevity is the use of a vacuum packer, such as the FoodSaver, to remove all oxygen from the bag and seal it properly.

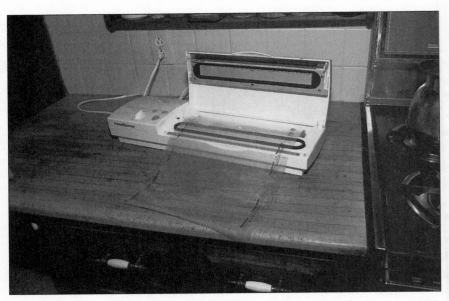

The first step is to create a bag of the appropriate size, using the roll bag material.

Meat is placed in the bag, and the machine automatically extracts the air from the bag and seals it.

bags should have a pattern of small air channels to ensure that air pockets don't form as the air is being removed.

It's important to choose the proper vacuum-packaging system. Bag sealers, sometimes thought of as vacuum-packaging systems, use a heated wire that welds the bag closed. They do not have any mechanism for removing air from the bag before sealing. Some bag sealers have a small rotary fan to extract some of the air out of the plastic bags before they are sealed. Some systems use polyethylene bags. Others provide sheets of plastic from which bags of different lengths can be made by "welding" the seams with a heated-wire bag-sealing mechanism. The fans in these models don't have enough suction to create a vacuum. The amount of air removed is comparable to using a straw to suck air out of the bag. The plastic will shape itself loosely to the contours of the food in the bag, but it will be obvious that air remains in the bag. The type of bag material and the strength of the seal will determine whether oxygen is able to reenter the bag.

Electric vacuum-packaging systems, such as the FoodSaver Professional II, eliminate exposure to oxygen. These systems extract the existing air in a variety of containers, including bags. The Food-Saver Professional II stores game in patented bags that keep food fresh 3 to 5 times longer and eliminate freezer burn.

Once a small package is vacuum packed, it stays fresh in the freezer for as long as 2 years. Large cuts of meat will stay fresh in the freezer as long as 3 years. Another plus is that vacuum-packaged meat takes up less space in the freezer because it doesn't have to be packed in water.

CHAPTER 6

Smoking and Drying Wildfowl

S moking and drying are excellent methods of preserving wild-fowl and are most often used with the less popular but more abundant birds, such as snow geese. Preserving meat by smok-ing involves the use of cold smoking; hot-smoke cooking is dis-cussed in Chapter 7.

WILDFOWL JERKY

Wildfowl can be dried as jerky or made into pemmican, but other types of meats are more commonly used for those foods. Making wild turkey, pheasants, and grouse into jerky is also pretty much a waste of great-tasting meat.

If you do wish to make jerky, here is a simple method: Trim away all the fat and as much connective tissue as possible from the meat. Then cut the meat into strips about ¼-inch thick with the grain, rather than across the grain. Combine the meat with Lawry's Sea-soned Marinade (or other bottled or packaged marinade) in a glass bowl or zippered plastic bag, and refrigerate for at least 2 hours.

You can also use the following ingredients to make your own marinade:

soy sauce
1 tablespoon garlic salt
1 tablespoon lemon pepper
1 tablespoon onion powder
Tabasco sauce (from a few drops to 1 or more tablespoons,
   depending on taste)
Water to cover

Wildfowl can be cold or hot smoked, using a variety of smokers.

Again, combine ingredients in a glass bowl or zippered plastic bag, and refrigerate 2 hours or overnight.

Remove the meat, shake the excess marinade from the strips, pat the meat dry, and sprinkle it with seasoned salt and garlic pepper. For spicier jerky, use the seasoned salt plus seasoned pepper or Cajun seasoning.

To dry the meat, place a sheet of aluminum foil in the bottom of your stove's oven to catch any drippings, and drape the meat over the oven racks, leaving enough space between pieces for the air to circulate. Spraying the oven racks with a cooking spray keeps the jerky strips from sticking. Set the oven to about 150°F, then crack the door open an inch or so. A dehydrator can also be used to dry jerky.

Most jerky will take 5 or 6 hours, but times vary depending on the heat of your individual oven and the thickness of the meat. Check for doneness after 3 hours, and remove pieces as they become dry.

The jerky should not be pink inside, but don't overdry game bird meat. Jerky is done when you can still bend it, overdone when

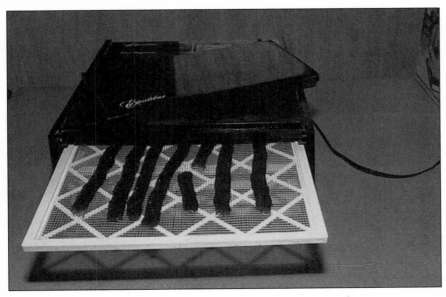

Use a dehydrator to finish drying jerky, after cooking it to 160°F.

it snaps. Store the finished product in a cool, dry place. Vacuum sealing also works well for storing jerky.

According to the United States Department of Agriculture (USDA) Food Safety and Inspection Service (FSIS), "When raw meat or poultry is dehydrated at home—either in a warm oven or a food dehydrator—to make jerky which will be stored on the shelf, pathogenic bacteria are likely to survive the dry heat of a warm oven and especially the 130° to 140°F of a food dehydrator." Following is their recommended methods of properly drying jerky:

Due to the possibility of illness from Salmonella and E. coli 0157:H7 from homemade jerky, the USDA current recommendation for making jerky safely is to *heat meat to 160°F before the dehydrating process*. This step assures that any bacteria present will be destroyed by wet heat. But most dehydrator instructions do not include this step, and a dehydrator may not reach temperatures high enough to heat meat to 160°F. After heating to 160°F, maintaining a constant dehydrator temperature of 130° to 140°F during the drying process is important because (1) the process must be fast enough to dry food before it spoils; and (2) it must remove enough water that microorganisms are unable to grow.

The USDA recommends the following safe handling and preparation methods:

—Always wash hands thoroughly with soap and water before and after working with meat products.

—Use clean equipment and utensils.

—Keep meat and poultry refrigerated at 40°F or slightly below; use or freeze ground meats and poultry within two days; whole red meats, within three to five days.

—Defrost frozen meat in the refrigerator, not on the kitchen counter.

—Marinate meat in the refrigerator. Don't save marinade to reuse. Marinades are used to tenderize and flavor the jerky before dehydrating it.

—Steam or roast meat and poultry to 160°F as measured with a meat thermometer before dehydrating it.

—Dry meats in a food dehydrator that has an adjustable temperature dial and will maintain a temperature of at least 130° to 140°F throughout the drying process.

JERKY SHOOTER

A better method of making jerky from wildfowl meat is utilizing ground meat run through a jerky gun, such as those from Cabela's and Bass Pro. These guns often come in a kit complete with the spices needed to mix with specified pounds of ground meat. This process makes jerky quick and easy. Grinding the meat also allows the use of smaller chunks of meat that might not be as readily utilized for sliced jerky. The jerky is extruded into strips or rolls, then dried in the same manner as sliced jerky; the strips have to lay flat, however. If using your oven as the dryer, extrude the strips or rolls onto any food-safe, washable screening, cheesecloth, or parchment paper and lay these on the oven racks to dry.

You can also make up your own ground jerky following the recipe below; however, you will still need a jerky gun to make the jerky strips or rolls.

5 pounds ground wildfowl game meat
5 heaping teaspoons Morton Tender Quick Salt
¼ cup brown sugar

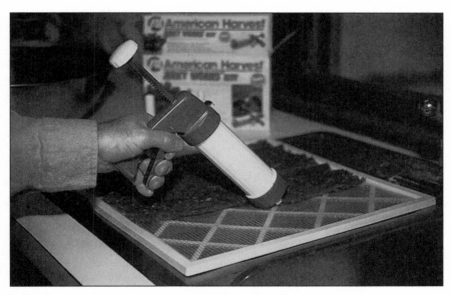

Jerky shooters let you make jerky quickly and easily.

1 teaspoon garlic powder
1 teaspoon onion powder
¼ to ½ teaspoon ground red pepper or ½ teaspoon dried red
  pepper flakes

Mix the spices together, then sprinkle over the ground meat and use your hands to mix together. Sprinkle a portion of the spices over the meat, mix that in and add more spices, mixing well after each addition. Again, spices and flavorings can be added to suit. As with any marinades, use a stainless-steel, enameled, glass, or plastic container. Cover the container and refrigerate at least 12 hours or overnight. Then press into jerky strips or rolls and dry as above.

COLD SMOKING

Larger birds, such as turkeys, can be brined and "cold smoked," but should still be kept refrigerated or frozen. Although cold smoking is a means of preservation, we no longer smoke dry meats for the time required to preserve them without refrigeration, but use the smoker to add flavor and then finish cooking in the oven. Cold smokers rarely exceed temperatures of 165°F. Cold smoking requires a cold smoker, such as the electric Little Chief Smoker from Luhr-Jensen. The Luhr-Jensen Little Chief Brand Home Electric Smoker is a simple metal box with racks to hold items for smoking. An electric plate in the bottom provides the heat, and a pan on the plate holds wood chips to provide the smoke.

The Luhr-Jensen Little Chief Smoker can be used for smoking, smoke flavoring, or drying, and comes with an instruction book that also includes recipes. The same smoker can be used to cure jerky and smoke sausages. The company also sells a wide assortment of brine and seasoning mixes, including the All-Purpose Brine and Upland Game Brine Mix, as well as different wood-flavor fuels, including hickory, apple, alder, cherry, and mesquite.

You can make up your own cold smoker from an old refrigerator. I've even used a large wooden box as a smoker in the past.

You'll also need a large refrigerator or cooler for the brining process, or you can brine during cold weather as the old-timers did. The brine temperature must be kept below 40°F but not freezing, which is why doing it outside can get complicated. The brine consists of 2 gallons of water, 1½ cups salt, ¼ cup sugar, ¼ cup brown sugar, 1 teaspoon onion powder, 1 teaspoon garlic powder, and ⅓ cup of soy sauce.

Place the thawed or fresh bird in a plastic, ceramic, or glass container, and cover it with the brine. The bird must be kept submerged. Use a plate and a clean weight, such as a plastic bag filled with water, to hold the bird down. Soak an average-size turkey in brine for 48 hours. Rearrange the meat after 24 hours, and stir the brine to keep it working and to assure that all parts are brined completely.

Fire up the smoker and bring the temperature up to 100°F. Maintain the temperature at 100°F and keep the wood-chip supply replenished. It will normally take about 36 hours to properly smoke a turkey. The skin will take on a deep golden, reddish-brown color. To ensure that the entire bird is thoroughly cooked, smoke it until the internal temperature of the center of the breast reaches 190°F, or "poultry done" on a meat thermometer. This may take quite a bit more time for a large bird. Another method is to smoke the turkey for about 24 hours or until golden brown, then finish cooking in a conventional oven. The bird should be wrapped in aluminum foil, and a bit of liquid or water should be added to avoid drying out the meat.

SMOKED SUMMER SAUSAGE

One great use of goose breasts and other wildfowl is smoked summer sausage. You can have a smokehouse make your sausage, mixing one-half lean pork with one-half wildfowl breast meat. If you have a grinder and cold smoker or smokehouse, you can make your own smoked summer sausage.

For 10 pounds of sausage, you need:

5 pounds wildfowl breast meat
5 pounds lean pork
6 tablespoons salt
1 tablespoon black pepper
4 tablespoons powdered dextrose
1 teaspoon ground mustard
1 teaspoon ground ginger

1 teaspoon ground coriander
6 teaspoon corn syrup solids
1 teaspoon garlic powder

Trim fat from the pork, then grind the goose and lean pork through a ³⁄₁₆-inch grinder plate. Cut the fat trimmings into ½-inch cubes. Mix all the ingredients in a plastic or stainless-steel bowl or container. Cover and place in a refrigerator for 48 hours. Regrind meat and fat chunks through a 3/16-inch grinder plate, and stuff meat into casings. The most commonly used casings are 2½ to 2¾ by 24-inch beef middles.

Hang sausages on smokesticks to dry at room temperature for about 5 hours. Preheat smoker or smokehouse to between 120°and 130°F. Place sausages in smokehouse, and maintain temperature for 3 to 4 hours. Then raise the temperature to 165°F and cook. The internal temperature on the sausages must reach 160°F. If you can't achieve an internal temperature of 165°F, then finish the process in your oven. When cooking is done, shower the sausages with cold water until their internal temperature drops to 120°F. Hang at room temperature for 1 to 2 hours, then place in a cooler for 24 hours.

More information about cold smoking—along with most of the supplies needed, including casings, grinders, and stuffers—is available from the Sausage Maker.

SNOW GOOSE SAUSAGE

The huge amount of meat that successful snow goose hunters can accumulate encourages innovations such as this easy-does-it recipe for snow goose salami.

12 pounds of snow goose meat
3 pounds of boneless pork
Morton Tender-Quick (1 tablespoon per pound of ground meat)
6 teaspoons Liquid Smoke (if smoked in a smoker, do NOT use
   Liquid Smoke)
5 teaspoons garlic powder
6 teaspoons cracked pepper
6 teaspoons whole mustard seed
2 teaspoons ground cayenne pepper
1 tablespoon crushed red pepper

Grind the meats together and mix with the spices. Use your hands to knead the spices into the ground meat. Cover and chill overnight. Divide into 1-pound portions and roll each into an 8-inch log. The easiest way to keep the logs approximately the same is to use a plastic bowl or a measuring cup. Pack the cup and dump for each log, then shape keeping the logs the same length. Wrap each log tightly with cheesecloth and tie the ends. Place on a wire rack over a pan and bake 4 hours at 225°F or until 165°F in the center. Freeze or refrigerate until used.

Note: The same recipe is also good stuffed in casings, smoked a few hours, then oven-baked at 225°F until the logs are 165°F in the center.

Note: This recipe also makes excellent goose jerky. The chilled meat can be made into jerky with the jerky shooter and dehydrated or oven dried as mentioned in the jerky section.

CHAPTER

7

Cooking Wildfowl

Most wildfowl is fairly lean, although some ducks and Canada geese can carry a heavy layer of fat. As with all game, removing excess fat is a first step in preparation for cooking. Make sure all blood, damaged meat, and shot is removed. The meat should be kept clean and properly cooled to maintain freshness and provide safe food.

Wildfowl can be baked, fried, broiled, boiled, grilled, or cooked in a slow cooker. Some birds require little in the way of flavoring; others require help from marinades and flavored sauces or spices.

Domestic birds are preconditioned by proper feeding to assure the same "quality" meats we have come to expect. However, quite often, game birds are what they eat. Most serious waterfowlers wouldn't consider eating coots or fish-eating mergansers, although recipes do exist for the hardy. Such ducks as mallards, gadwalls, and teal, on the other hand, are relished for their good taste because they are primarily vegetarians, feeding mostly on food sources such as rice, corn, acorns, and seeds.

The condition of the birds is also important. They may be fat or lean, healthy or unhealthy. Birds that are noticeably unhealthy or diseased should be discarded. In many public waterfowl areas where crippling regularly occurs, birds that cannot fly or swim properly should not be taken for food.

Age in some birds is also important. As most upland birds have relatively short lives, age is not a problem with them. Old geese or turkeys, on the other hand, can be quite tough.

Wildfowl is best eaten while fresh, and proper care should be taken to field dress and maintain their freshness. The meat of most wildfowl—even an old goose with lots of fat on the outside—is relatively dry. Wildfowl should not be overcooked, although it should be cooked to done or "poultry done" stage.

SMOKE COOKING AND SMOKE FLAVORING

Smoke cooking, or hot smoking, is an excellent method for cooking wildfowl, from quail to turkeys. Smoke cooking or hot smoking is cooking with a high heat while simultaneously adding smoke. Smoke cooking or barbecuing is a southern tradition. In fact, look behind any barn or shed in my part of the Ozarks, and chances are you'll find a homemade smoker. A variety of reliable, easy-to-use cookers and smokers may also be found on the market.

Three types of smoke cookers are available. The first type is the simple barbecue grill, charcoal or gas. You either pile on the charcoal briquettes or light the gas and cook with the heat. Charcoal adds some smoke flavor, and wood chips can be added to the charcoal or to the rocks of most gas grills for added smoke flavoring. The second type of smoke cooker uses a high dome with a lid and a separate pan to hold marinade. Moistened wood chips are added for smoking. A number of these are available, including models from Cabela's, Brinkman, Coleman, and Bass Pro Shops. Both of these smokers cook by direct heat.

True smokers, however, are quite often larger models made of welded metal to maintain consistent heat and are capable of handling much more fire as well as more meat at one loading. They cook by indirect heat, with the coals in one area of the smoker and the meat in another. A number of these smokers are available, but the best I've tested is the Good-One Grill and Smoker from Ron Goodwin Enterprises. The Good-One is available in several sizes, from small to large commercial models. All are built with the same basic design. The front lower compartment is the firebox and grill. You can grill just as you would with any charcoal grill. The upper back compartment, however, is for smoking or cooking meats with lower, indirect heat. On the lower front of the firebox are the air-control dampers to control the heat in the firebox and grill area. On the top of the smoker lid is an exhaust vent. The heat in the smoker is controlled by the dampers. The smokers are constructed with a clean-out pan located under the firebox grate.

To smoke, the top grate is removed from the bottom compartment and charcoal placed on the bottom grate. You'll need about 10 pounds of charcoal for several hours of smoking. After the coals are burning well, add the wood chunks to provide the smoke flavor and close the bottom lid. Just as in any smoking, the type of wood chunks used provide the flavoring. These types of smokers do not use water pans. "Water pans make steam heat, which can cause smoke to disappear rapidly and tends to make meat soggy," said Ron Goodwin. "We don't recommend water pans for true, old-fashioned pit barbecue flavor." Goodwin also suggests using pure charcoal chunks rather than briquettes, although the former are a little harder to obtain. "Another secret to good barbecue smoked meat is a smoker that will hold an even temperature and the right amount and kind of wood," he added. "Hickory, mesquite, oak, pecan, alder, and fruit woods—such as cherry, peach, apple, or grape vine—are recommended. Poultry requires much less wood than other meats, and game birds and waterfowl are very good if smoked with fruit woods. The best smoke flavor comes from using two or three chunks of wood, about 3 to 4 inches in size."

Maintaining an even temperature over a long period of time is important for ease in smoke cooking. The Good-One smoker has a temperature gauge and a variety of means of regulating the heat. You can control the heat precisely by simply opening and closing the dampers. You will also need a meat thermometer to check the internal temperature of your meat.

Smoke cooking is an excellent method for cooking wildfowl, from pheasants to turkeys to geese and ducks, because it keeps the moisture in the meat rather than drying it out. Even an extra-dry goose comes out moist and, for the most part, tender.

My friend, Bill Harper—game-call manufacturer, lecturer, outdoor television personality, former owner of a barbecue restaurant, cookbook author, and producer of barbecue seasoning and sauces—has the following technique for cooking wild turkey on the Good-One. "Pluck the turkey, then cut off the legs at the joints. Rub the turkey with cooking oil thoroughly inside and out. Then rub my seasonings really heavy inside and out and smoke 6 to 8 hours at 225° to 250°F or until the internal temperature is 185°F." It's a simple recipe even the first-time smoke/cooker will appreciate.

You might like Harper's cranberry juice marinade. For this recipe, he prefers to skin the turkey, remove the legs and thighs, and split the turkey breast down the center. He suggests cooking and deboning the legs and thighs for use in other recipes.

"Soak the breast halves overnight in a cranberry marinade," Harper says, "consisting of 1 quart of cranberry juice, ¼ cup soy sauce, ½ cup cooking oil, ½ teaspoon rosemary, 1 tablespoon sweet basil, 1 tablespoon of Bill Harper's Seasoning, and ½ cup brown sugar.

"Place the turkey halves with meat side up, rib cage down, and lay bacon strips over the breasts to add moisture. Smoke at 225° to 250°F until a meat thermometer in the breast reads 185°F. This will probably take about 5 hours. I usually cook for about 4 hours, then wrap the breasts in foil because it makes the meat juicier. One thing you want to remember about smoking is that you're only going to get so much smoke flavor into the meat, then it just begins to dry out. Incidentally, this recipe works great for ducks and geese as well."

Goodwin suggests the following for ducks, geese, and game birds. "Cook 50 to 60 minutes per pound at a temperature of 225° to 250°F. When done, baste with sauce, cut the temperature back to 150°F, and hold for serving. If you don't serve within 1 hour, wrap it in foil."

Regardless of the bird, I prefer to smoke for about an hour or 2, then wrap the bird in foil for the remainder of the cooking process. This tends to hold in more moisture. The birds can be basted with barbecue sauce, left natural, or basted with lemon pepper and butter or a marinade of your choice.

Smoking wildfowl is fun. Because their meat is rich and succulent to taste, they can be eaten hot from the smoker, or they can be made into hors d'oeuvres and cold snacks. You'll find your culinary reputation soaring when you serve smoked pheasant with mild cheese, crackers, and a dry white wine.

One New Year's Eve, we decided to forgo the sit-down dinner we've held for a long time, and instead smoked pheasants, ducks, geese, and trout, which we then offered along with other snack-type foods. Not only was the evening much easier on the hosts, but our guests raved about the great-tasting wild-game foods. You can smoke any number of foods, including hors d'oeuvres such as meatballs, franks, shrimp, eggs, and cheese.

The following recipes are for smoke-flavored birds from the Luhr-Jensen Little Chief home electric smoker recipe book. It's a good idea to marinate the larger birds, as the curing agents tend to tenderize the meats, and the juices, herbs, and spices tend to color and tone the taste of the birds. Smaller wild birds with a more delicate flavor often don't require marinades.

Cherry-Flavored Duck

3 young ducks, halved or quartered
1 cup red wine
1 teaspoon fresh ginger
1 teaspoon dry mustard
⅓ cup brown sugar

Trim off fat. Smoke flavor ducks for 2 to 3 hours in the Little Chief Smoker using cherry wood for flavor. Remove ducks from the smoker and marinate them in a mixture of the above ingredients overnight. Barbecue until done, 45 to 60 minutes. Baste with marinade while broiling.

Pecan-Stuffed Smoked Pheasant

¼ cup butter
1⅓ cups dry bread crumbs
⅔ cup coarsely broken pecan meats
2 pheasants

To smoke pheasants,
brine:
¼ cup water
¼ cup soy sauce
¼ cup brown sugar
¼ cup dry white wine
½ tsp. onion powder
½ tsp. garlic powder
½ tsp. ground ginger

Place the birds in the cool brine for 6 hours. Rinse and dry on paper towels for 1 hour. Smoke with two pans of Hickory Flavor Chips n' Chunks for 2 to 4 hours. Remove from smoker, prepare suffing by combining pecans, bread crumbs, and melted butter. Stuff pheasant and truss.

Combine

2 tbsp. flour
¾ tsp. salt
¼ tsp. pepper

and lightly sprinkle over pheasant.

¼ cup butter
1½ cups hot water
⅓ cup sherry

Melt butter in a heavy frying pan. Brown each pheasant on all sides and transfer to a roasting pan. Add hot water and sherry to the browned birds. Cover and bake at 350 degrees for 1 hour. Baste with liquid every 15 minutes. Remove cover and continue baking for 20 minutes, or until the birds are crisp and brown. Remove birds to a platter and keep hot while you thicken drippings for gravy. Serves 6.

GRILLING WILDFOWL

Some wildfowl can be grilled or direct-heat barbecued; some can't. Mesquite-grilled quail are a favored and elegant food in many parts of Texas, and grilled quail combined with grilled shrimp will make anyone drool. Even with this type of barbecue, it's best to grill the birds on a grill that has two burners. Flash-grill the birds over direct heat for about 2 minutes per side, then switch to the side with the burner off and continue grilling. Birds grilled in this manner are best without barbecue sauce in my opinion. I do sprinkle a little garlic powder over them and provide a coating of butter before grilling. It takes only a few minutes to grill most wildfowl—except for turkeys, of course.

Grilled Snow Goose

Snow geese are relatively small, averaging 6 to 8 pounds of live weight. Most hunters use a fillet knife to slice off breast meat into two boneless steaks. One bird yields about a pound of dark, rich breast

Grilling is also a great way of cooking most wildfowl.

meat. Marinating is a frequent choice for preparation. One quick and easy recipe calls for soaking breast fillets in Italian salad dressing and then quick cooking over a hot charcoal fire or in the broiler. Another variation uses equal parts of white cooking wine and soy sauce seasoned with fresh garlic, ginger root, and fresh lime juice.

For best results, perforate the fillets with a fork and allow to marinate overnight. Wrap breast halves in smoked bacon to prevent drying and check often to prevent overcooking. The red color of the meat makes it easy to underestimate doneness. Cook only until firm in the center, leaving the fillets juicy and tender. Combine pan drippings with leftover marinade to make a sauce and serve with wild rice.

Another grilling method for goose breast is a favorite of our son, Mark, who does a lot of waterfowl hunting and eating. Mark cuts the breast meat with the grain into fingers. The fingers are marinated several hours or overnight in a mixture of bottled barbecue sauce laced with red wine. Add salt, pepper, garlic, or favorite spices. Grill over coals, basting in additional barbecue sauce—the spicier, the better.

Wildfowl Recipes

Wildfowl recipes can be simple or the ultimate in gourmet cooking. Over many years of wildfowl hunting, our family has tried many recipes for all types of wildfowl from upland game to waterfowl and wild turkeys. Following are some of our favorites as well as a wide variety of tried-and-true recipes from friends and also from hunting camps we've had the pleasure of visiting. Don't be afraid to try wildfowl cooking in your kitchen or backyard. You may discover some new family favorites.

UPLAND BIRDS

Grilled Pheasant Fingers

Another recipe from friend and hunting companion, Dr. J. H. Thies. Jerry often prepares these for a before-dinner treat, especially in the warmer months when gatherings are outside on the deck and these treats can be served directly from the grill.

Boned breast from pheasants cut into lengthwise fingers about ½ inch by 2 inches long. Marinate the fingers 4 to 6 hours in Doc Pete's Marinate.

When the guests have arrived, place the fingers on the grill. Use any grill topper to keep from dropping the fingers through the grill; a stir fry or fish topper works great, or carefully lay the fingers across the grill.

Grill exactly 4 minutes on one side, turn over and grill exactly 3½ minutes on the other side. Serve immediately.

Pheasant and Dressing

2 pheasants, breasts deboned
1 box cornbread stuffing mix
1 can cream of mushroom or golden mushroom soup
1 soup can milk or part sour cream
Seasoned flour
Oil

Slice each pheasant breast in half lengthwise to make eight pieces. Dip each in salt-and-pepper-seasoned flour, and brown in oil. Prepare the stuffing mix according to package directions, and spread it in a greased 9 × 13 glass baking dish. Top stuffing with the browned pheasant, and spread the soup-milk mixture over it. Bake at 350°F for approximately 1 hour or until the pheasant forks tender and the top is brown.

Serve with a salad and warmed rolls.

Note: This recipe can be prepared early in the day and refrigerated, then baked for the evening meal. Be sure to add at least 15 minutes to the baking time, and do not preheat oven. Put the cold glass dish into a cold oven and let both warm at the same time.

Sherried Pheasant

Breast from two pheasants
2 tablespoons butter or margarine
1 medium onion, chopped
1 small can sliced mushrooms
1¾ cups water
2 cups instant brown rice
2 teaspoons dried parsley
Bacon slices
Salt and pepper
½ cup dry sherry
¼ cup melted butter

Sauté onion in butter until transparent. Salt and pepper pheasant breasts, and brown on both sides, adding more butter if needed. Remove breasts. Add mushrooms and liquid, water, and parsley to skillet. Bring to a boil, and add instant rice. Cook and stir a few minutes, then cover tightly and remove from heat until liquid is absorbed. Spread rice into a large buttered casserole dish and top with browned pheasant breasts. Arrange bacon slices over pheasant. Roast, uncovered, in a 350°F oven for 1½ hours or until pheasant is tender. Baste often with the melted butter and sherry mixed together. Remove bacon slices before serving.

Rough Creek Lodge Pan-Roasted Pheasant with Sweet Onion Risotto

Rough Creek Lodge Executive Retreat and Resort, located in Glen Rose, Texas, is the ultimate in resorts and offers some of the best Texas quail hunting, along with some of the most exquisite wild game dinners I've experienced. The words on their brochure say it all: "Redefining unique, luxury hotels, resorts and clubs." Not only can you meet, hunt, and fish at Rough Creek, but Chef Gerard Thompson offers several opportunities to earn your own "chef" hat by participating in such courses as "Cooking with Edible Flowers," "Grilling Techniques for Entertaining at Home," and "The Chef and I." Thanks to Chef Gerard Thompson for sharing several of his recipes.

Pan-Roasted Pheasant

6 fresh pheasant breasts (6–8 ounces each)
1 tablespoon chopped fresh thyme
½ cup grape seed or olive oil
Kosher salt
Freshly cracked black pepper

Preheat oven to 400°F. Place pheasant breasts in a bowl, and add thyme and oil. Generously season with salt and pepper. Heat a large sauté pan over high heat, and let it just start to smoke. Sear and roast pheasant breasts two at a time on both sides until golden brown— about 5 minutes. Transfer the pheasants to an ovenproof pan and, when all are seared, roast in oven 5 to 8 minutes. Remove from oven and let rest at room temperature for 5 minutes before slicing.

Sweet Onion Risotto

1 Texas sweet onion
½ cup unsalted butter
2 cups Italian Arborio rice
½ cup white wine

Pheasant from Rough Creek. Once the bird is in the kitchen, the options are limitless.

8 cups hot chicken broth
1 tablespoon lemon zest
½ cup Reggiano Parmesan cheese
Kosher salt
Freshly cracked black pepper

Peel, slice, and chop the onion. Heat ¼ cup of the butter over low heat in a heavy-bottomed pot. In a separate pot, warm the chicken broth and keep it warm. As the butter begins to melt, add the finely chopped onion, and cook slowly for 12 to 18 minutes or until golden brown. Stir frequently to be sure onion caramelizes and does not burn. (This may be done to this point up to 1 day ahead.) Add rice and cook for 2 minutes. Add white wine and cook until wine has absorbed. Turn heat up to medium, and set your timer for 15 minutes. Begin to add warm chicken broth, 1 cup at a time. Season with salt and pepper. Let the rice absorb each cup before adding the next.

Be sure to constantly stir the rice so it does not stick. At this point, the rice should have a creamy consistency. When the timer sounds, stir in the other ¼ cup of butter, lemon zest, and the Parmesan cheese. To serve, immediately divide among six plates. Slice pheasant and place on top of risotto.

Suggestion: Sauté ½ cup pancetta with three bunches of Swiss chard as an accompaniment.

Rough Creek Lodge Grilled Pheasant with Grilled Romaine Lettuce and Tomato Caper Relish

Pheasant Marinade

1 tablespoon balsamic vinegar
1 shallot, finely diced
1 cup vegetable oil
2 cloves garlic, chopped
1 tablespoon chopped fine thyme
Zest of 1 lemon
Salt
Cracked black pepper
4 pheasant breasts (6–8 ounces each)

Mix all ingredients and let marinate 4 hours. Remove from marinade, and grill over charcoal 5 to 7 minutes on each side or roast in oven for 15 minutes at 350°F.

Caesar Dressing

⅛ cup sherry wine vinegar
⅛ cup fresh lemon juice
2 garlic cloves, chopped fine
1 tablespoon Dijon mustard
2 teaspoons Worcestershire sauce
8 anchovy fillets, minced
3 egg yolks
1 cup olive oil
¾ cup Romano cheese
Salt and black pepper to taste

In a mixing bowl, combine the sherry wine vinegar, lemon juice, garlic cloves, Dijon mustard, Worcestershire sauce, anchovy fillets, and egg yolks. Whisk until frothy. Continue to whisk while slowly adding the olive oil. Season with salt and cracked black pepper. Fold in ½ cup Romano cheese, and save the other ¼ cup for finishing the dish.

Tomato Caper Relish

2 cups tomatoes, diced and seeds removed
1 cup sun-dried tomatoes, diced
¼ cup capers
¼ cup basil, chopped
¼ cup olive oil
½ cup roast garlic, chopped (but not fine)
½ cup Kalamata olives, pitted and quartered
Salt and cracked black pepper

Mix all ingredients together.

Grilled Romaine Lettuce

1 large head romaine lettuce, cut in four wedges
1 tablespoon olive oil
1 lemon
Salt and pepper

Drizzle lettuce with olive oil and lemon. Season with salt and pepper, and grill over hot charcoal.

To plate: Place 2 to 3 ounces Caesar dressing on bottom of plate. Place (now hot-grilled) romaine wedge in center of plate. Slice (now roasted) pheasant on plate, and sprinkle with tomato-caper relish and Romano cheese.

Lemon Pheasant

2 pounds of pheasant breast, cut into ½ inch cubes
Flour
Salt and pepper
Oil

Coat the breast meat with seasoned flour and fry in hot oil until done. As the pieces are cooked, remove to a warm platter and keep warm.

Sauce

½ cup fresh lemon juice
1½ cups water
¾ cup sugar
Cornstarch
One or two drops yellow food coloring

Bring lemon juice, water, and sugar to a boil and thicken with cornstarch. Add a drop or two of yellow food coloring. Gently stir the warm meat into the sauce and serve over rice.

Pheasant Parmigiana

Breast from one pheasant, sliced into ¼-inch thick cutlets
1 egg, slightly beaten
¼ cup Parmesan cheese
1 cup Italian bread crumbs
Olive oil
1 can or jar spaghetti sauce
Mozzarella cheese, thin slices or shredded

Mix the Parmesan cheese and Italian bread crumbs. Dip the breast cutlets in egg and then in the bread crumb mixture. Brown the cutlets in a small amount of olive oil, turning once. Place the browned cutlets in a single layer in a baking dish or large saute skillet, pour the spaghetti sauce over and around the cutlets and place a slice of mozzarella cheese or a small amount of shredded mozzarella on each cutlet. Bake at 350 degrees or heat in the skillet on the stovetop until the sauce is warmed and the cheese melted. Serve over fettuccini.

Pheasants à la Dobbins

This recipe (and several others) came from the late E. Ragland Dobbins, a fine Southern gentleman; his son, Scrappy; and his grandson, Kent, who have all been long-time hunting companions and friends.

2 pheasants
4 cups water
½ cup vinegar
4 cups chopped celery
2 medium onions, quartered
4 to 6 whole cloves
½-inch cinnamon stick
5 teaspoons sugar
1 teaspoon salt
2 bay leaves
Salt and pepper
½ cup butter

Cut pheasant breasts in half or whole pheasants into serving-size pieces. Combine water, vinegar, celery, onions, cloves, cinnamon, sugar, salt, and bay leaves in a large bowl. Marinate pheasants in mixture for 12 hours, turning occasionally. Remove pheasants and dry well. Reserve marinade. Sprinkle pheasants with salt and pepper, and brown in hot butter in large skillet. Add 2 cups of marinade, and simmer covered for 1 hour, adding more marinade during cooking if necessary. Yield 4 servings.

Dobbins Flattened Quail in Wine

2 quail per person
Flour
Oil
Salt and pepper
1 medium onion

1 cup white wine
1 cup chicken broth

To flatten quail, start by removing the backbone just below the rib cage on both sides. This can be done with a very sharp boning knife or a good pair of poultry shears. Turn the quail breast side up, and press down with the palm of your hand. Expect some of the rib bones to break. Salt, pepper, and flour the quail. Brown quail in a large skillet with oil at medium heat. Slice onion, divide it into single rings, and place over quail. Add wine and broth. Simmer in a tightly covered skillet for 45 minutes or until tender, turning occasionally.

Rough Creek Lodge Hot-Smoked Quail with Sherry-Maple Glaze

Marinade

1 lemon, zested
1 shallot, finely chopped
2 garlic cloves, finely chopped
1 teaspoon fresh thyme, chopped
¼ cup sherry vinegar
½ cup olive oil
Salt
Cracked black pepper

Glaze

½ cup maple syrup
½ cup sherry vinegar

Reduce until syrup consistency.

Quail

4 fresh quail
1 tablespoon Rough Creek Lodge chili seasoning

Marinate the quail for 1 hour. Season with chili seasoning and grill, adding your favorite smoking chips to the fire. Place quail on plate and drizzle with a small amount of the glaze.

Mesquite-Grilled Quail (with Skillet Wild Rice)

This recipe is a particular favorite of the Burch clan.

Mesquite-Grilled Quail

Quail, skin removed, split lengthwise (one breast and one leg)
Italian dressing

Marinate quail overnight or all day in Italian dressing. Grill over mesquite chips approximately 3 minutes to a side. Baste with Italian dressing while cooking. Serve with Skillet Wild Rice.

Skillet Wild Rice

1 package long grain and wild rice (6.2 ounces, regular or fast cook)
2 cups water
½ cup chopped sweet green pepper
½ cup chopped sweet red pepper
1 medium onion, chopped
2 tablespoons butter or margarine

Brown peppers and onion in butter in a heavy skillet that has a tight lid. Add water and bring to a boil. Add rice and seasoning packet and stir. Cover with tight lid, lower temperature, and simmer until rice is done, stirring occasionally. *Note:* This can also be placed in the oven.

Country-Fried Quail with Gravy

Quail, skin removed, split lengthwise (one breast and one leg)
Seasoned flour
Oil
Milk
Salt and pepper

Roll each quail in seasoned flour and fry in oil over medium heat. Watch closely and turn as needed. These cook quickly. Remove quail to a heated platter and keep them warm. Stir flour into the pan drippings, then add milk and cook until thickened, stirring constantly. Add salt and pepper as needed. Serve with mashed potatoes, buttermilk biscuits, and lots of gravy.

O So Good BBQ

Some of the best cooking I've enjoyed on my many hunts was in the Maine hunting camp of Kathie and Scott Lee of Oxyoke Originals, makers of muzzleloading accessories. Regardless of whether hunting bear or moose with black powder, the meals are always sumptuous at their hunting camps. O So Good BBQ is a favorite, and Kathie says it's quick and easy to serve a full camp of hunters.

For each 2 pounds of meat, preferably quail—
1 cup Lea & Perrins barbecue sauce, or your favorite
2 tablespoons Worcestershire sauce
1 to 2 tablespoons cognac
1 onion, sliced
1 red pepper, sliced

Mix the barbecue sauce with the Worcestershire sauce and cognac. Spread over the meat and place the onion and red pepper slices over the top. Bake 1 hour or slow cook over an open pit fire until tender.

Chef Eric's Poached Quail in Vegetable Broth

From Lawry's Foods, makers of many fine seasonings and marinades used for wildfowl, comes this recipe for Poached Quail. This recipe was developed by Chef Eric A. Widmer, a contributing chef to Lawry's Foods and a finalist in the 1994 National Game and Game Fish Cook-off.

12 quail with rib cage and thighbone removed
1 cup Lawry's Mesquite with Lime Juice Marinade
¼ teaspoon black pepper
½ pound bacon, diced
1 onion, diced
2 stalks fresh fennel, cored and sliced
2 quarts chicken stock
1 bay leaf
2 small russet potatoes, peeled and thinly sliced
1 8¾ ounce can kernel corn
1 leek, sliced
2 cloves garlic, minced
Lawry's Seasoned Salt
White pepper

In resealable plastic bag, combine quail, Mesquite with Lime Juice Marinade, and black pepper. Seal bag and refrigerate 2 hours. In large stock pot, saute bacon and onion until onions are caramelized. Add fennel, chicken stock, bay leaf, and marinated quail. Simmer, uncovered, 50 minutes or until quail are tender. Remove quail from stock; set aside. Add potato and corn to stock. Simmer, uncovered, 5 minutes. Add leek, garlic, Seasoned Salt, and white pepper, to taste. Simmer, uncovered, an additional 3 to 4 minutes. Makes 6 servings.

Presentation: Place 2 quail in serving bowl. Add stock and vegetables, about 1½ cups, distributing vegetables as evenly as possible. Drizzle with Red Bell Pepper Sauce.

Red Bell Pepper Sauce

1 14 ounce jar roasted red bell peppers
½ teaspoon Lawry's Garlic Powder with Parsley
¼ cup Lawry's Mesquite with Lime Juice Marinade
2 limes, cut into wedges (garnish)

In blender, combine red bell pepper, Garlic Powder with Parsley, and Mesquite with Lime Juice Marinade. Blend on medium for 15 to 30 seconds.

South of the Border Doves

This recipe is from *Cooking Wild Game and More* by Bill Harper, a longtime hunting buddy and wild-game cooking expert.

½ cup diced onion
½ cup diced green chilies
¼ cup butter
1 pound dove breast fillets
1 cup flour
1 teaspoon cumin
⅛ teaspoon oregano
1 teaspoon chili powder
1 teaspoon Bill's Seasoning
Splash of Tabasco Sauce
1 large can chopped or stewed tomatoes
1 tablespoon Bill's Seasoning

Saute onions and green chilies in 2 tablespoons butter. Remove and set aside. Roll doves in flour mixed with 1 teaspoon Bill's Seasoning. In the skillet brown doves in remaining butter. Add onions and green chilies and remaining ingredients. Simmer 30 minutes or until tender. Serve over rice.

Dobbins Slow-Cooked Dove Breasts

20 to 30 skinned dove breasts
2 cans cream of mushroom soup with roasted garlic
Hearty red wine

Fill an electric slow cooker halfway with dove breasts; most will hold 20 to 30. Combine 2 cans of soup with same amount of red wine and pour over dove breasts. If not completely covered, add more wine. Cover tightly and cook on low for about 6 hours. Serve with wild rice. Reserve the sauce to pour over dove and rice.

Grilled Dove

This is the first recipe we remember using for dove when we set up housekeeping a good number of years ago. Although it has evolved a bit over time, it is still a favorite.

Dove breasts
Onion
Bacon
Italian dressing

Marinate dove breasts in Italian salad dressing several hours or overnight. Place a chunk of onion inside each breast and wrap in bacon, securing end with a toothpick. Grill over hot coals until tender, basting with Italian dressing and turning often. Be careful not to overcook.

Thayne's Charcoal Chicken

From Thayne and Joan Smith, long-time friends and Kansas hunters, come several recipes for their favorite bird: the prairie chicken. Thayne says this charcoal chicken is the very best and that the recipe is also their favorite way of cooking dove and duck breasts. It works well on any dark-meat bird.

Prairie chicken breast fillets
Bacon
Olive oil
Cavender's All-Purpose Greek Seasoning

Slice prairie chicken breast fillets in two to three strips, depending on the size of the bird. Roll each strip in a slice of bacon, preferably hickory-smoked bacon, and hold in place with small skewers or toothpicks. Dip each strip in olive oil, completely covering each, and place in a glass dish. Liberally cover on all sides with Cavender's All-Purpose Greek Seasoning, and place in refrigerator for several hours. Cook slowly on barbecue grill with hickory added for flavor until done. Note that the strips will turn dark brown or black on the grill, but this is no indication they are burned or overcooked.

Thayne's Prairie Chicken Casserole

Smith notes that this recipe works well with pheasant, sage grouse, quail, and partridge, as well as the prairie chicken.

4 to 5 filleted prairie chicken breasts
Flour
Shortening for frying
1 can cream of chicken soup
1 tablespoon onion salt
½ cup diced celery
½ cup diced carrots
1 can (4 ounces) mushrooms
½ cup melted butter
Salt and pepper

Remove meat from chicken breasts with a sharp knife, then cut each half into two or three fillets. Flour each, and brown in hot shortening. Place browned pieces in two layers in a casserole dish with the remaining ingredients. Bake covered for 1½ hours at 325°F. Remove cover for last 15 minutes.

Thayne's Prairie Chicken and Broccoli Quiche

This is good even if you don't like broccoli.

1 whole prairie chicken, skinned

4 cups of water
1 bunch fresh broccoli, chopped
1 9-inch pie shell, homemade or purchased
1 cup shredded Swiss cheese
4 green onions, diced (including tops)
3 eggs, beaten
1 cup heavy cream
½ cup milk
Salt and pepper
¼ cup grated Parmesan cheese

Combine prairie chicken and water in a stockpot. Parboil meat for 45 minutes. Remove chicken from water and allow to cool. Press pie shell into 9- × 13-inch baking dish or in quiche dish. Steam broccoli in one cup of water. Drain and set aside. Debone prairie chicken and dice meat into small chunks. Combine meat, chopped broccoli, Swiss cheese, onions, eggs, cream, and milk in a large mixing bowl. Salt and pepper to taste. Mix well. Pour mixture into quiche or baking dish and sprinkle Parmesan cheese on top. Place in oven and bake for 45 minutes at 350°F or until knife inserted in center comes out clean. Remove from oven and let stand for 5 minutes. Serve hot.

Dutch-Oven Woodcock

6 to 8 woodcock breast fillets
Flour
Salt and pepper
Oil
2 packages dry onion soup mix
2 cups water

Salt and pepper breast fillets, coat with flour, and brown in oil. Remove fillets from Dutch oven as they are browned. Stir 2 to 3 tablespoons flour into pan drippings, then add soup mix, and slowly add 2 cups water. Stir to dissolve soup mix, and return woodcock fillets to pan. Place the lid on the Dutch oven, and lower the heat. Simmer 1 hour or until fillets are tender. The Dutch oven can also be baked in the oven or cooked over coals.

WILD TURKEY

Deep-Fried Wild Turkey

Probably the most popular method of cooking turkey today is deep frying it in a special turkey fryer. My good friend, the late Ben Lee, was deep frying turkey breast long before the method became popular. His method used a fish fryer and oil heated until a paper match on the bottom of the cooker burst into flames. Then he added the turkey breast and cooked it until brown.

To cook, follow the directions with your turkey fryer. Most recipes call for injecting the turkey with seasonings with a special injector kit. Dry rubs can also be used to add more spice, and Cajun flavoring is one of the most popular. King Kooker recommends that you first determine the amount of oil needed in the pot. Do this by placing the turkey in the pot and adding water to just cover the bird. Remove the turkey from the pot and measure the water. Remove the water, and add the same amount of peanut oil to the pot. Light the cooker as per instructions, always use a deep-fry thermometer to monitor the temperature of the oil, and never let the oil temperature exceed 350°F. Thaw, then towel dry the turkey. Make sure no ice crystals remain. Coat the turkey with King Kooker Cajun Seasoning and inject with marinade. Place the turkey on the frying rack with the legs up. Using mitts for protection and the lifting hook, lower the turkey into the 350°F oil very slowly. Be careful not to splash hot oil. Cook turkey at 350°F for 3½ minutes per pound. When the planned cooking time has passed, turn off the gas and check the turkey for doneness. Make sure the burner is off before lifting the turkey. Using mitts and a lifting hook, slowly lift the turkey from the pot. Check for doneness by slicing at the thigh joint; if the thigh appears to be well cooked, the turkey is ready. Allow the turkey to sit for 20 to 30 minutes before carving.

Always use caution when cooking with hot oil. King Kooker also warns to never use their product inside, only outside on a non-combustible surface. Never leave your outdoor cooker unattended. If a grease fire should occur, turn off the gas and cover the pot.

Deep frying is the culinary rage.

Bag-Roasted Wild Turkey à la Thanksgiving

The following recipe is a Thanksgiving tradition at the home of Jerry Thies, a long-time friend and hunting companion.

Thies cleans the bird by scalding and plucking. He boils 5 gallons of water on the stove, then pours it into a large cooler. Thies says the cooler works well, as it keeps the water hot while more is boiling and is large enough to totally immerse the bird. After scalding, he plucks the bird and removes the entrails, keeping the liver, gizzard, and heart.

The next step is to fill the cavity of the bird with chunked apples, onions, and celery. Add salt and pepper (and rosemary, if desired), and place in a domestic turkey roasting bag. Thies stresses that the key to success with this baking method is to follow the time recommended on the cooking bag for the turkey weight, but to cook ½ hour less for wild turkey.

While the turkey is roasting, chop the giblets in ¼-inch cubes and sauté. Use the giblets to make gravy. Cook dressing separately, using some of the sautéed giblets and fat. Thies makes dressing from seasoned bread cubes, and he prefers Italian flavor. Grandma Thies always added raisins to dressing.

Open the cooking bag for the last ½ hour of cooking, and let the turkey brown. Discard apples, onions, and celery before serving. Thies says a fresh turkey is best for this recipe, but frozen is okay, as it still has that wild nutty flavor.

Baked Wild Turkey with Dressing and Gravy

One whole, plucked wild turkey
Salt and pepper
1 cup butter or margarine
Water

Clean the turkey inside and out and pat dry. Rub the inside of the bird with butter, then salt and pepper the inside. Place the bird, breast side down, on the rack of a deep roasting pan or electric roaster. Add water to the roaster until the breast is covered, adding approximately 1 teaspoon salt per quart of water used. Rub exposed bird with butter and put remaining butter in the broth. Salt and pepper the exposed turkey back and cover tightly. Bake at 325°F for approximately 4 hours or until tender.

Dressing

1 small package corn muffin mix, baked according to package directions and crumbled (or use one package cornbread stuffing mix)
1 1-pound loaf white bread, cubed
½ pound mild or hot pork breakfast sausage
1 large onion, diced
4 to 6 stalks celery with leaves, diced
4 eggs
Poultry seasoning
Salt and pepper

Mix the crumbled cornbread and cubed white bread and let air dry for an hour or so. Brown the sausage with onion and celery. Drain excess fat.

About an hour before dinner, add the sausage mixture to the bread mixture and season with poultry seasoning, salt, and pepper. Beat 4 eggs with wire whip and add to mixture. Gradually add hot broth dipped from around the cooking turkey. Add slowly and stir with each addition so the eggs aren't cooked with the hot broth. Add broth until the mixture is liquefied but still very thick. Pour into a well-greased baking dish or iron skillet. Bake at 350°F until set in the center.

Remove the turkey about ½ hour before dinner. Let cool slightly, debone, and move meat to serving platter. Slice breast meat and add to platter.

Gravy

Pour remaining broth into a saucepan. Add chopped giblet, and thicken with flour shaken or wire whipped with water. Cook over medium heat, stirring often until gravy is slightly thickened.

Serve with mashed potatoes and your favorite holiday fare.

Turkey and Noodles

Turkey legs and thighs
1 egg
2 tablespoons milk
½ teaspoon salt
1 cup flour

Place turkey legs and thighs in a stock pot and cover with salted water. Simmer until the meat falls from the bones. Strain broth and return to pot. Remove meat from the bones and add the meat to the broth.

Prepare the noodles while the turkey legs and thighs are cooking. With a wire whisk stir together the egg, milk, and salt. Stir in enough flour to make a stiff dough (about 1 cup). Roll on a floured board or cloth until very thin. Allow to dry ½ hour, then roll and cut into ¼-inch strips. Unroll strips and spread out to dry for an hour or so. Noodles can also be made without the milk by using 2 whole eggs or several egg yolks.

Drop strips a few at a time into the boiling broth and cook about 10 minutes.

Turkey Cacciatore

Breast fillets from one turkey
Seasoned flour
Oil
1 medium onion, diced
2 cloves garlic, minced
1 green pepper, diced
1 or 2 bay leaves
2 teaspoons Italian seasoning
2 14.5-ounce cans diced tomatoes
1 8-ounce can tomato sauce
Fettuccine
Parmesan cheese

Slice turkey breast into steaks or cut into finger strips. Roll in seasoned flour and brown in a skillet in oil. When fillets are browned on both sides, remove from skillet and keep warm. Brown onion, garlic, and pepper in skillet. Stir 1 tablespoon seasoned flour into drippings in skillet, and add canned tomatoes with juice, bay leaves, and Italian seasoning. Simmer until reduced and thickened. Add tomato sauce and adjust seasonings. Carefully place cooked fillets into sauce and cook over low heat another 15 to 20 minutes. Serve over fettuccine and pass the Parmesan cheese. Remove bay leaves before serving.

Quick Cacciatore

Prepare turkey as above. Pour your favorite bottled spaghetti sauce around the browned turkey fillets in the skillet. Simmer together 5 to 10 minutes to blend flavors. Serve over fettuccine, and pass the Parmesan cheese.

Smothered Turkey Breasts

Breast fillets from one turkey
Garlic salt
Lemon pepper
1 can cream of mushroom soup
1 soup can of milk
1 package dry onion soup mix
1 cup sour cream
1 small can sliced mushrooms, drained

Pat turkey breast fillets dry and sprinkle both sides with garlic salt and lemon pepper. Place in a greased baking dish large enough for the two breast pieces to lay flat. Blend the soups, milk, and sour cream together using a wire whisk, stir in the drained mushrooms, and pour over the fillets. Bake covered for 45 minutes in a 350°F oven. Uncover, spoon sauce over fillets, and continue baking until tender and browned slightly. Serve sliced with sauce.

This recipe is also good prepared the day before. The breast meat is chilled and thin sliced, then warmed in the sauce before serving.

Chicken-Fried Turkey Steak

Turkey breast
Salt and pepper
Flour
1 egg
½ cup milk
Oil

Thinly slice the turkey breast across the grain into cutlets. Salt and pepper meat, and flour. Pound the flour into the meat with the edge of a plate or side of a meat mallet. Flour and pound both sides of the meat. Let the meat sit a few minutes until the flour is absorbed. Blend egg and milk together and dip cutlets in mixture, then in flour again. Let sit a few more minutes, then fry in hot oil in a cast-iron skillet. Fry each cutlet until golden brown on both sides. Remove cutlets to a warm platter, and keep warm while making gravy. Pour excess oil from skillet, leaving a small amount of oil with the pan scrapings. Stir flour into these scrapings until all oil is absorbed. Slowly add milk, and heat and stir until thick. Add salt and pepper as needed, and more milk if the gravy gets too thick. Serve cutlets with mashed potatoes and gravy and, of course, buttermilk biscuits.

Barb's King's Ranch Turkey

This recipe started out as King's Ranch Chicken. When we were served this dish at the home of friends, Jim and Barb Gardner, I had to have the recipe. But because our freezer has more wild turkey and pheasant than chicken, we soon converted it to wild meats.

Layer the following in this order, in a greased, deep 9 × 13 pan (or two 8-inch pans, and freeze one for later):

Slightly crushed corn or nacho chips
Diced or sliced cooked wild turkey or pheasant (leftover meat or stewed legs, thighs, etc.)
1 can condensed cream of mushroom soup diluted with ½ soup can cooking broth or chicken broth
1 cup each of chopped onion and chopped sweet pepper sautéed in ¼ cup margarine and 3 tablespoons water
Slices of Velveeta cheese to cover (only Velveeta works)
½ teaspoon garlic powder, evenly sprinkled
1 can condensed cream of chicken soup diluted with ½ soup can cooking broth or chicken broth
1 can diced tomatoes and green chilies (Rotel)
1½ teaspoons chili powder, evenly sprinkled

Bake at 350°F until bubbly, about 35 to 45 minutes. Serves 8 generously. Can be extended into an even larger pan with more turkey and extending the soups with 1 soup can of broth. Serve with salad and garlic bread.

Wild Turkey Strips

If your family likes the local fast-food version of chicken strips, they will love this.

Turkey breast
Salt and pepper
Flour
1 egg
Small can of evaporated milk
Oil

Cut the turkey breast with the grain lengthwise into 1-inch strips. Partially freezing the meat makes slicing much easier. Beat egg with evaporated milk and mix salt and pepper with flour. Pat strips dry, then dip in egg mixture, roll in flour, and place strips on waxed paper. When all the strips have been dipped, start over with the first strips done. Redip in egg mixture and roll in flour again.

Heat ½-inch oil in a heavy, deep skillet and begin frying with the first strips dipped. Turn once and cook until browned. These don't take very long to fry and become hard and tough if overcooked. *Note:* These strips can also be cooked in a fish fryer or other deep fryer, making it much easier to serve several people or a crowd.

Eddie Salter's Southern Style Turkey Fingers

Here's another version of turkey strips, a favorite recipe of long-time hunting friend Eddie Salter. Salter is a Hunter's Specialties pro staffer.

Turkey strips
Eggs
Buttermilk
Seasoned flour
Peanut oil

Marinate turkey strips in egg and buttermilk for an hour. Spread seasoned (salt and pepper) flour on waxed paper, and roll the fingers in the flour. Deep fry in peanut oil at 375°F until the pieces float. Drain and serve with your favorite dip, such as barbecue sauce or honey mustard sauce.

Eddie Salter's Grilled Turkey Rolls

Turkey breast
Italian dressing
Greek salad peppers or sweet cherry peppers
Bacon

Cut turkey breast into strips approximately ½-inch thick, as wide as three fingers, or about 3 inches wide and about 6 inches long. Marinate the strips in Italian dressing for 1½ hours. Wrap the strips around Greek salad peppers or sweet cherry peppers and then wrap a strip of bacon around each and secure with a toothpick. Cook about 20 minutes on a very hot grill. Start cooking the strips over the coals, then move to an aluminum-foil-covered section of the grill or, on a two-burner grill, move the rolls to the off side before the bacon begins to flare. These are excellent!

WATERFOWL

Blind Duck

This comes from my long-time hunting buddy, Jim Spencer of Arkansas Game & Fish, a recipe he learned from Mike and Dave Meseberg, of Mar-Don Resort on Potholes Lake in Washington. "Because it's such a long run from the lodge to the hunting area, the Mesebergs feed their hunters in the duck blind," said Spencer. "Sandwiches are a staple, of course, but one of the nice little touches they employ is a simple recipe they call 'Blind Duck.' It's simple shish-kebab, really, but it was the first time I'd seen it done the way they do it—atop a five-gallon metal charcoal bucket half filled with sand, which they use for a primitive in-the-blind heater.

"Before you start on me, I know that a charcoal bucket probably isn't the healthiest type of heater you can put in a duck blind. But if you stay out of the fumes coming off the thing, and if your blind isn't closed up entirely, it's not going to kill you. If you want to give Blind Duck a try in your blind or pit, here's how:

"First kill a duck or two and fillet the breasts. (Be sure to save the rest of the carcass with the head and/or wings intact, to keep from running afowl of the law. Cube each breast into smaller pieces; the way Mike and Dave do it, one side of a mallard breast

A brace of wood ducks, the makings of an excellent meal.

makes about 10 pieces, a gadwall or wood duck about 7. Sprinkle the pieces generously with your favorite seasoning. Mike and Dave swear by Luhr Jensen's Waterfowl Seasoning and lemon pepper, and it's hard to argue with their results, but I'm partial to Cavender's Greek Seasoning. Plain old salt and pepper would work just fine.

"Whatever you use, when you're through sprinkling it on the ducks, skewer them on dried, smooth-barked sticks (willow works great, but switch-cane, sycamore, cottonwood, or hickory would do just as well), separating the meat chunks with two- or three-inch square pieces of bacon. Leave those wimpy tomatoes, onions, and other vegetables at home; this is a recipe for carnivores.

"While you've been cutting and skewering, the charcoal in your bucket should have been cooking down some. Lay the skewers across the top of the bucket and keep on watching empty skies, swapping lies with your hunting buddies and daydreaming. Turn the skewers occasionally, and when they look ready to eat, dig in. This recipe takes about a duck to feed each hunter. If you use a charcoal bucket to heat your duck blind, give Meseberg's Blind Duck a try. If you don't use a charcoal bucket, this is a good reason to start."

Martha's Stuffed Duck "Pot Roasted"

This recipe is a specialty of the Hackberry Rod and Gun Club, Hackberry, Louisiana, and comes from their *Secret Cook Book*. Hackberry may just be heaven—where else can you shoot a limit of waterfowl in the morning and catch a limit of specs or reds in the afternoon? Terry and Martha Shaughnessy, owners of Hackberry, note that this is the only way they have found to completely tenderize ducks or geese and remove all the wild flavor. Martha suggests serving over wild or white rice with gravy from ducks and with sweet potatoes and rolls.

Cleaned ducks or geese
Pan sausage (half mild and half hot mixed together), enough to stuff cavities
Tony Chachere's Creole Seasoning
Olive oil
Fresh mushrooms, sliced
2 to 3 tablespoons Kitchen Bouquet (browning and seasoning liquid)
Water (to almost cover ducks)
Cornstarch dissolved in water

Stuff cavity of birds with sausage and sprinkle Creole seasoning on outside. Brown in olive oil on top of stove, turning often, until very dark. Place in heavy iron pot, and pour water to almost cover birds. Add mushrooms and Kitchen Bouquet. Bring to a gentle boil and cover with tight lid. Simmer until meat falls from the bones (3 to 5 hours). Remove birds and thicken gravy with cornstarch.

Mark's Best Duck

My son Mark, who kills and eats more ducks than anyone else I know, thinks this is the only way to prepare duck breast. They are always tender and delicious, no matter what kind of duck or what its age might be.

Duck breast fillets
Flour
Salt and pepper
Oil
2 cans cream of mushroom soup
1 to 2 cans milk

Pound fillets into duck steaks. Cut fillets from larger ducks lengthwise into two pieces, then pound. Salt and pepper each fillet, then coat in flour. Brown in oil, turning once. Place fillets in a 9 × 13 baking dish. Mix milk and soup and pour over fillets to cover. Bake in a 350°F oven about 1 hour or until fillets are tender. Serve with broth over rice, noodles, or mashed potatoes.

Pan-Fried Duck Breasts

Duck breast fillets
Flour
Oil
1 package dry onion soup mix
1 onion, sliced
Water

Pat dry duck breast fillets. Slice larger breasts lengthwise into two thinner fillets. Dip fillets in flour and brown in oil. Remove fillets and drain on paper towel. Separate onions into rings and brown in oil. Drain excess oil from the skillet and stir two tablespoons flour into drippings. Add dry onion soup mix and 2 cups water. Stir to dissolve soup mix, and place fillets on onions. Cover tightly and simmer 30 minutes or until duck breasts are tender. Add more water if needed. Delicious with potatoes or rice.

Dobbins Wild Goose with Orange Sauce

1 wild goose
Salt
2 to 3 apples, quartered
2 to 3 onions, quartered
1 cup butter
6 tablespoons orange juice concentrate
½ cup dry sherry

Parboil goose for 20 minutes in salted water. Salt cavity and stuff with apples and onions. Bake at 350°F for 1 hour. Combine butter, orange juice concentrate, and sherry to make orange sauce. Reduce oven to 225°F. Cover pan with foil or lid and bake 2 more hours. Remove the lid for the last 30 minutes to brown. Baste throughout cooking with orange sauce, keeping remainder of sauce warm on stove top. Serve sauce with goose.

Quick Orange Duck

Breasts from two large or three small ducks
6 ounces orange juice concentrate
½ stick butter or margarine, or more as needed
Salt and lemon pepper

Pat dry breast meat and sprinkle with salt and lemon pepper. Melt butter in a large skillet over a medium heat, add duck breasts, and brown both sides. Add orange juice concentrate, cover tightly, and lower heat. Simmer until tender, turning breasts often to glaze. Serve over rice, pouring orange glaze over all.

Dobbins Roast Duckling

2 ducks (about 4 pounds each)
1 medium carrot
1 medium onion
3 stalks celery
½ pound bacon
½ cup sliced green olives
½ cup sliced black olives
1 cup sliced mushrooms
½ cup sherry wine
1 teaspoon thyme leaves
½ cup chicken broth
Salt and pepper
Cornstarch

Rub ducks with salt, pepper, and thyme inside and out. Chop carrot, onion, and celery, and place in body cavity. Roast ducks at 325°F for 2½ hours. Remove and save vegetables. Let the ducks cool, and split down the middle. Remove breastbones and backbones. Pour all grease from pan. Chop and sauté bacon until crisp; drain. Put bacon, mushrooms, olives, and vegetables in roasting pan. Brown. Add sherry and chicken broth and bring to a boil. Thicken with a little cornstarch. Place ducks in sauce and simmer for 10 minutes before serving. Serve with wild rice.

Sweet and Sour Duck

Breast of 1 large or 2 small ducks
Oil
2 to 3 carrots, sliced
½ to 1 sweet green pepper, cut in strips
½ to 1 sweet red pepper, cut in strips
1 15 ounce can pineapple chunks, drained, liquid reserved
1 8-ounce can sliced water chestnuts
Soy sauce
¼ cup cornstarch

Pat dry the duck breast and cut into ½-inch cubes. Stir the cornstarch and soy sauce together and add the meat. Stir until all the
meat is coated. Prepare the vegetables. In a wok, deep fry the
breast pieces a few at a time. Remove all but two tablespoons of the
oil and brown the carrots. Start with a few slices and as they brown,
push them up the sides and add more carrots to the oil in the center
of the wok. When the carrots are slightly tender, add the peppers.
When the peppers and carrots are tender, stir in the drained pineapple chunks and water chestnuts. Stir in the meat pieces.

Sweet and Sour Sauce

¼ cup catsup
¼ cup sugar
1 Tablespoon cornstarch
1¼ cup reserved pineapple juice, add water if necessary
1 teaspoon vinegar

In a small sauce pan, blend the cornstarch and sugar and stir in the
pineapple juice. Blend in the catsup and vinegar. Cook and stir until
sauce thickens. Pour over the meat and vegetables and stir to coat.
Serve over rice.

Hot and Spicy Wildfowl Soup

1 goose or duck carcass, without skin
1 onion
1 stalk celery
Salt and pepper or peppercorns

Place the carcass in a stock pot with the vegetables and cover with water. Add salt and pepper or peppercorns. Simmer over low heat until the meat falls from the bones. Discard vegetables. Strain broth and return to the stock pot. Dice the meat and add to the strained broth. Add the following to the broth:

1 14.5 ounce can diced tomatoes
1 small can chopped green chilies
1 sweet green pepper, diced
1 medium onion, diced
1 can whole kernel corn

Simmer until the vegetables are tender. Adjust seasoning, adding bottled pepper sauce or another can of green chilies if you prefer more heat.

Flour tortilla strips
Fine shredded cheddar cheese

Roll a flour tortilla and cut into ¼ inch strips. Place on a baking dish and bake in a 350 degree oven for 5 to 10 minutes or until lightly brown. Garnish each bowl of soup with the tortilla strips and a little shredded cheddar cheese. Serve with corn chips or cheese crackers.

Bobby and Guy's Pit Cooked Duck Breast

This recipe from the *Hackberry Rod and Gun Club's Secret Cook Book* could be a Southern version of Blind Duck, but would be equally good cooked at home over the grill.

Cleaned duck breasts
2 to 3 slices of jalapenos per duck breast
Bacon slices, uncooked
Tony Chachere's Creole Seasoning

Fold each duck breast in half, placing 2 to 3 slices of jalapenos in the breast. Wrap with slice of bacon and sprinkle with Creole seasoning. Place duck breasts on preheated pit. Do not overcook, best when slightly pink in the middle.

Roast Goose with Dressing

This is an excellent recipe for Thanksgiving or Christmas dinner and calls for a large, plucked goose.

1 package dressing mix: chicken, turkey, or cornbread flavor
1 package long grain and wild rice
1 large or 2 small oranges, pared and sections chopped
1 cup cranberries, chopped in food processor or blender
Salt and pepper

Mix together the prepared dressing mix and wild rice mix and stir in the orange sections and cranberries. Remove excess fat from the goose, rub the cavity with salt and pepper, and stuff with the dressing mix. Place breast side up on a rack in a roasting pan. Cover tightly with lid or foil and roast at 325°F for 2 hours. Remove excess fat from roaster and return to oven for 1½ hours, or until browned and tender or meat thermometer inserted in breast registers 195°F. Baste often during the last hour with 1½ cups orange juice blended with ½ cup orange marmalade.

Roast Goose with Fruit Stuffing

This is another excellent holiday recipe and, again, calls for a large, plucked goose.

1 package dressing mix: chicken or turkey flavor
1½ cups diced pared apple
½ cup chopped onion
½ cup chopped celery
1 tablespoon butter or margarine
½ cup raisins
Salt and pepper
4 thick slices bacon

Sauté onion and celery in butter. Prepare dressing mix according to package, adding the apple, onion, celery, and raisins. Remove excess fat from the goose, rub cavity with salt and pepper, and stuff with the dressing mix. Place breast side up on a rack in a roasting pan. Cover tightly with lid or foil and roast at 325°F for 2 hours. Remove excess fat from roaster. Lay half slices of bacon across the breast. Return to oven, and baste often with pan drippings. Roast until browned and tender or meat thermometer inserted in breast registers 195°F. Remove bacon slices before serving.

Barbecue-Stuffed Snow Goose Breast

This recipe is from the *Snow Goose Cookbook,* published in Churchill, Manitoba, and available through the Arkansas Game and Fish Commission. This recipe was sent in by Pat Kehoe of Brooks, Alberta.

8 snow goose breast fillets
5 slices bacon, diced
2 stalks celery, diced
1 medium red onion, chopped
1 green pepper, chopped
¼ red pepper, chopped
½ cup cheddar cheese, shredded
½ cup mozzarella cheese, shredded
¼ cup steak sauce

Fry bacon until translucent. Add chopped vegetables and cook until slightly softened. Add steak sauce and simmer 5 minutes. Remove and cool. Slice each goose breast along one side to create a pocket. Stuff the fillets with the vegetable mixture and the cheese. Seal with toothpicks. Barbecue until meat is medium rare. Serve with rice, French fries, or baked potato.

Poached Duck Breast

Breast of 2 large or 3 small ducks
Salt and pepper
1 stick butter or margarine
2 tablespoons Worcestershire sauce
2 tablespoons current jelly
2 cups red table wine
2 tablespoons cognac

Pat dry breast meat and sprinkle with salt and pepper. Melt butter in large skillet, add duck breasts, and brown on both sides. Remove from skillet, stir in remaining ingredients, and return ducks to skillet. Poach ducks in the wine sauce until tender. Serve with wine sauce over rice or fettuccine.

Wildfowl Kabob

Dice any wildfowl breast meat into 1-inch cubes, and marinate overnight in Italian salad dressing. Alternate meat cubes with pearl onions or quartered onion, chunks of green or red pepper, and whole, small mushrooms onto skewers. Grill, turning often and basting with Italian dressing. Do not overcook. Serve with wild rice.

Wildfowl Gumbo

Preparing wildfowl gumbo is (at least) a 2-day affair. There are as many different recipes for gumbo as there are ingredients—this is just one version. If you don't already have a favorite gumbo recipe, start with this one, and you will soon have it adapted to suit your family.

Wildfowl
Salt and pepper
1 cayenne pepper (or 1 teaspoon crushed)
2 or 3 bay leaves
1 stalk celery
1 carrot
1 medium onion
2 cans diced tomatoes (with or without green chilies)
3 stalks celery, diced
3 cloves garlic, diced
2–3 medium onions, diced
1–2 green peppers, diced
1 tablespoon Italian seasoning
Creole seasoning or red pepper
⅓ cup oil or butter
1 cup flour

Optional:

Corn
Lima beans
Carrots
Vegetables
Gumbo filé
1 package frozen cut okra
1 pound chopped fresh fish fillets or fresh seafood

Fill a large stock pot with whole ducks or geese or a combination. You might also use just legs and thighs from a variety of wildfowl, including turkey and pheasant. Once you've tried this, you'll be sure to freeze special bags of legs and thighs just for gumbo. Cover with water, adding approximately 1 teaspoon salt and 1/2 teaspoon pepper per quart of water used to cover the fowl. Also add one hot cayenne pepper (or more if you're brave), the bay leaves, celery stalk, carrot, and medium onion to the pot.

Cook until the meat is easily removed from the bones. Debone meat and chop. Strain broth and press the vegetables through the sieve. Refrigerate meat and broth overnight.

The next morning, remove any fat from the broth and pour the broth and meat into a stock pot or large Dutch oven. Add the diced tomatoes, diced celery, diced garlic cloves, diced onions, diced green peppers, Italian seasoning, and Creole seasoning or red pepper to taste. You can also add corn, lima beans, carrots, or vegetables to suit, as well as 1 teaspoon to 1 tablespoon fresh gumbo filé or to suit. Simmer 1 to 2 hours, stirring often.

In a cast iron skillet, make a roux of the oil or butter and flour. Cook over low heat until well browned, stirring constantly.

Adjust seasonings in the gumbo. Add roux to thicken. Add one package frozen cut okra (optional), and 1 pound chopped fresh fish fillets or fresh seafood of your choice. Simmer another 30 minutes. Stir, but try not to break up the fish or seafood. Serve in large, flat (pasta-type) bowls over rice.

Rough Creek Lodge Game Bird Pot Au Feu

The success of this dish will depend on fresh birds. Frozen birds will not give the same results. Serves 4.

2 whole fresh dove or squab
1 whole 2.5- to 3-pound fresh pheasant
1 pound duck sausage, cut into 4 pieces
2 boneless Texas quail, cut in half
2 tablespoons vegetable oil, for cooking the birds

Sauce

2 plum tomatoes, each cut into 4 pieces
1 onion, rough chopped
1 carrot, rough chopped